Past-into-Present Series

FARMING

R. D. Lobban

Printed in Great Britain by
Redwood Press Limited, Trowbridge, Wilts.
for the publishers
B. T. Batsford Ltd, 4 Fitzhardinge Street, London, WC1V OAH

Acknowledgment

The author and Publishers would like to thank the following for the photographs used in this book: The Bodlean Library for fig. 11; Anne Bolt for fig. 62; *British Farmer* for fig. 49; The British Museum for figs 3 and 16; BP Ltd for fig. 59; Cambridge University Department of Aerial Photography for figs 7, 13 and 22; *Farmers' Weekly* for figs 41, 48, 55, 57, 58, 60 and 61; *The Field* for fig. 2; Ford Motor Co for fig. 53; Fox Photos for figs 50 and 64; IAEA for figs 1 (Dincer) and 65; ICI Ltd for fig. 54; The Imperial War Museum for figs 47 and 51; KLM for fig. 63; the Mansell Collection for figs 30, 31, 32, 34, 36, 37, 38 and 52; *Radio Times* Hulton Picture Library for fig. 43; Ransomes Ltd for fig. 56; Reading University Museum of English Rural Life for figs 25, 26, 27 and 29; The Science Museum for fig. 44.

Contents

The Illustrations

1 The First Farmers

One of Man's greatest needs is for food, and throughout the centuries the farmer has played a most important part in the life of any community. Even today with all our nuclear power, rockets and spacecraft, we could not survive for long without the food supplied by the world's farmers. If some disaster caused them to cease growing their crops or rearing their livestock, then quite swiftly our towns and cities would come to a standstill, and our whole civilisation would collapse.

Up until about 10,000 years ago men did not grow crops, nor did they have domesticated animals. In the main they were hunters, and hunted wild animals with sticks and stone weapons. They cooked the meat of the animals they killed, used the skins for clothes, and made the bones and horns into tools and weapons. They also supplemented their diet with plants, fruits and berries.

The First Herdsmen

Somewhere before 6,000 BC these early men began slowly to change their way of life until they were transformed from hunters into herdsmen and farmers. It is almost impossible for us to know exactly how all this took place, for men at this time did not write and leave records, but it is probable that they began to tame and domesticate animals which hung around their camps or settlements. The first such animal was most probably the dog, in those days a fierce wolf-like creature. They would hang around the camps for bones and scraps of meat, and gradually some of them would become tame and part of the life of the camp. Soon these dogs would help the men in their hunting for wild animals.

Dogs were not of course livestock, in the sense that people would eat them, but about the same time men began to tame animals that could provide them with a regular food supply. The first animal so domesticated was the sheep, and this first occurred in that part of the Middle East now known as Iran. Herds of wild sheep roamed around in this area, and groups or tribes of men began to follow them from pasture to pasture, just as the North American Indians in the nineteenth century followed the buffalo. They would hunt them for their meat and skins, and at the same time they would keep wild animals away from the herd.

Gradually as the years passed the men would gain more and more control over the herds until they were able to lead them and direct their movements. In this way, somewhere about 5,000 BC, several tribes in the Middle East changed from being hunters preying on the herds of sheep to shepherds caring for, and making the fullest possible use of their flocks. These tribes would still follow a nomadic existence, however, and their lives might have resembled those of the Old Testament shepherds as they led their flocks from one pastureland to another.

One animal which was domesticated in this same part of the world was the cow. But where we can quite easily picture the process whereby the herds of wild sheep were domesticated, it is much more difficult to understand how these early wild cattle were tamed. They were extremely fierce, and according to Julius Caesar they were almost as large as elephants. Some idea of their size can be gathered from the fact that men often made their horns into drinking cups. It must have required great courage and skill to tame such animals, but nevertheless, despite all the difficulties, cattle had been domesticated by about 4,000 BC.

Other animals which were domesticated at a relatively early date in the Middle East were the goat and the camel. The horse was first tamed somewhere to the north in the grasslands of Central Asia, while the pig was tamed in south-east Asia. In India men domesticated a wild fowl which became the ancestor of our modern hens.

Thus men in different parts of the world began to gain more control over the animal kingdom, and in the process many tribes became herdsmen and shepherds. The first herdsmen were nomads, wandering from pasture to pasture, and they lived in collapsible and transportable skin tents. Their principal means of livelihood were their flocks, for the animals supplied them with food, clothing, tools and dwelling places.

1 Algerian herdsmen, whose way of life has changed little for thousands of years, share a well with a modern technician, who is taking water samples for analysis

Cultivation of Crops

The next great advance in the history of agriculture came when men began to sow and cultivate crops. Again we have no exact knowledge of just how this came about, but we do know that certain grasses, the ancestors of our modern barley, oats and wheat, grew wild. Some tribes discovered that these grasses could be eaten, and as early as 6,000 BC they began to cut them with primitive sickles. The first sickles were made of bone and had a row of sharp flints inserted in a groove along the blade. They were straight like knives, but later it was discovered that curved sickles were much better for cutting standing grasses.

While men were reaping the wild grasses, many seeds must have fallen to the ground, and these would grow and produce crops the following year. In the course of time a few observant individuals would notice what was happening, and they would plant a few of the seeds. In this way the first farmers deliberately planted and cultivated their crops.

2 An auroch—the earliest type of European cattle which became extinct in the seventeenth century, but was later reproduced by special breeding

Ancient Egypt

Many men in different parts of the world seem to have made the discovery that seed could be planted to produce crops, but it was probably in the Nile Valley in Egypt and possibly in the other great river valleys like the Tigris, the Euphrates and the Indus that farming first developed on a fairly large scale. Each year the River Nile overflowed its banks, leaving behind it after the floods had subsided large deposits of mud. This mud was very fertile, and by about 5,000 BC the Egyptians were growing crops of wheat and barley on it.

The earliest farmers had discovered that their seed would grow better if the soil was disturbed and turned over before they were planted. At first this was done with pieces of stone, but the Egyptians soon invented a wooden hoe. This was shaped rather like a capital A, one arm being the blade and the other the handle. A piece of flint and later of copper was fixed to the end of the blade to act as a cutting edge. The farmer held the handle in his two hands and turned over the earth by jabbing the sharp point of the hoe into the ground and pulling it towards him.

Somewhere about 3,000 BC this hoe was transformed into a plough when the handle was lengthened so that it could be dragged along by two or three men and later by oxen. The new implement merely scratched the surface of the ground

3   A wooden model of a plough from Ancient Egypt

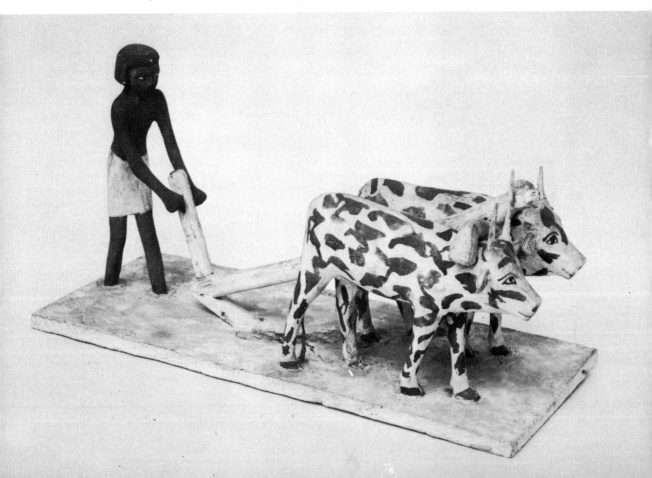

and did not turn over the soil completely, but nevertheless this was one of the most important developments in the history of agriculture. The modern plough is really only an improved version of this old Egyptian plough, and it is still one of the basic implements of farming today.

The Egyptians soon also discovered the importance of irrigating their fields. Their main source of supply was the Nile, for the climate of Egypt was dry and there was not enough rainfall to water the crops. The level of the fields was above that of the river, however, and the Egyptians had to find some means of raising the water. To do this they invented the *shaduf* and the Egyptian wheel.

The *shaduf* was a relatively simple device consisting of one horizontal pole balanced on top of another upright pole. At one end of the horizontal pole was a leather bucket, while on the other end was a ball of dried mud. The farmer pulled down the bucket, filled it with water, and then swung it up and emptied it into a channel flowing away through the fields. The weight of the mud ball on the other end of the pole acted as a counter-balance, and thus the farmer could lower the bucket and raise it full without any great effort.

4 Irrigating the fields by means of a *shaduf*

The Egyptians also invented a rather more complicated instrument, known as the Egyptian wheel, for irrigating their fields. This consisted of a large horizontal wheel with projecting wooden teeth which fitted into the wooden teeth of a second vertical wheel. Connected to this vertical wheel on an axle was a third wheel round which ran a rope, and to the rope at regular intervals were tied a number of baked clay pots. An ox was harnessed to the horizontal wheel and driven round in a circle all day. The horizontal wheel drove the vertical wheel and the axle, and thus the chain of pots moved endlessly up and down, full of water when going up and emptying into a channel leading to the fields.

Among the many other devices developed by the Egyptians to aid their farmers was the saddle quern. This was a flat stone on which the grain was laid, and a

5 Sculpture of a woman servant grinding corn in Ancient Egypt

sausage-shaped stone which was rolled backwards and forwards on the grain till it was ground into flour. The Egyptians also had ovens for baking bread, and they had learnt how to make leavened bread. The paste of wheaten flour and water was allowed to stand for some time in the open air, and as it did so the yeast spores acted upon it and caused the mixture to rise.

The development of farming in the Nile valley completely transformed the way of life of the Egyptians. Where before they had been nomads, they now began to live settled lives in farms and in villages. Later they became such efficient farmers and produced such large quantities of foodstuffs that they were able to support a huge population living in towns and cities near the Nile. Great temples, palaces and pyramids were built, and in Egypt there developed one of the most important civilisations of the Ancient World. All this was made possible by the first farmers who had learnt to cultivate the rich soil of the Nile valley.

Many of the finest aspects of Egyptian life and civilisation arose out of their system of farming. The study of geometry, for instance, was first developed in Ancient Egypt to meet the needs of agriculture. When it overflowed its banks each year, the Nile obliterated the boundaries of the fields. It therefore became necessary to mark out the boundaries year after year, and so a system of land measurement was evolved. In the same way the need to calculate the quantity and value of the grain harvest led to the development of arithmetic.

The beginning of the study of astronomy, too, was closely associated with the practise of agriculture. The Ancient Egyptians required some means of knowing when to expect the arrival of the annual flood waters so that they could prepare their dykes and irrigation systems, and this led them to watch the stars. By careful observation they discovered that when the star Sirius could be seen on the horizon at dawn then they could expect the Nile flood to reach the head of the delta. This in turn enabled the Egyptians to invent the first calendar, for they noticed that there were 365 days between the successive occasions when the star Sirius was in this particular position.

Another sphere where agriculture had a direct influence was in the development of an alphabet in Ancient Egypt. Early Egyptian writing is known as hicroglyphics and consisted of a combination of letters and word pictures. The letter A had one leg longer than the other, and it is most probable that this was in effect a picture of the Egyptian plough. This may well explain why the Greek and Latin words for ploughing start with 'a' and why our words agriculture and arable also begin with this letter.

And thus it was that in Egypt and in other lands men had completely altered their way of life by developing new methods of farming and domesticating wild animals. They were now able to produce enough to support great towns and cities, and their skill in farming the land had helped build up a wonderful civilisation and culture. Without doubt, therefore, those imaginative individuals who had planted the first seed and cultivated the first crops were among the great pioneers of the World's history.

2 Early Farming in Britain

While the important developments in farming and agriculture were taking place in Egypt, the early inhabitants of Britain were still living as hunters. About 3,000 BC, however, a new group of people moved across the English Channel and settled in the lands north of Salisbury Plain. They brought oxen, sheep, pigs and a dog like a fox-terrier with them, and they built large earthen stockyards to protect their herds. They also cultivated crops of barley, wheat and flax, but many of them lived a nomadic life and moved from pasture to pasture with their herds. Perhaps they cultivated a few fields and returned in the autumn to harvest the crops.

The Celts

For the next 2,000 years or so a number of other peoples arrived in Britain from the Continent, and they, too, lived a semi-pastoral and semi-nomadic way of life. Then about 1,000 BC the pattern of farming began to change with the arrival of a people known as the Celts. They had originally hailed from the Upper Danube in Austria, and they occupied Britain for over a thousand years till the arrival of the Anglo-Saxons. From their language, modern Welsh is derived, and many of their beliefs and customs still live on in ceremonies and superstitions concerning May Day and mistletoe.

During their occupation of Britain the Celts introduced the use of bronze and iron into the country. They had a light plough, but since it had no mouldboard they ploughed their lands along and across to make sure the soil was well turned over. The areas they settled and farmed were usually the lighter and higher grounds such as the Downs and the chalk hills of Sussex.

Many of the Celts had their own individual farms, and they cultivated the land in small square fields. Their main crops were wheat, oats and barley, and in addition to the oxen, sheep and pigs of earlier times they had also brought with them short horn cattle. They had small horses for transport and to pull their chariots.

The Celts were efficient farmers, and they introduced several important improvements in agriculture. They dug deep storage pits to hoard their grain, and erected raised granaries that were rat-proof. They produced more corn than they required for themselves and were able to export substantial quantities to the Continent. In return, they imported luxury goods, and a flourishing trade developed. Thus it was that the Celts, by their skill in faming, were able to achieve a fairly high standard of living and to build up a fine civilisation.

The Romans

In the first century BC, the Celts, or Britons as they were then being called, found themselves faced with a serious threat from across the Channel. The Romans had built up a huge Empire, and about 58 BC they began the conquest of Gaul (now France). There they learnt of the rich corn supplies in Britain, and in 55 BC and 54 BC the famous general Julius Caesar led an expedition over to Britain. Troubles within the Empire occupied the Romans for a time, but about a hundred years later, in AD 43 the Emperor Claudius landed with an invading army. Soon the Romans had conquered large parts of the country, but they found it difficult to hold Scotland and so they withdrew into England. They built Hadrian's Wall from the Tyne to the Solway, and for nearly 400 years England formed part of the great Roman Empire.

The Romans introduced further changes in farming. They built many important towns in Britain, and these created a large demand for grain and other food supplies. Other parts of the Empire also needed grain from Britain, while the army also needed to be fed. All this brought about the cultivation of larger areas of the country, and the total food production in Britain increased very considerably.

6 Traces of Celtic fields in Dorset

The Romans also introduced several new plants into Britain. Among these were the cherry, the vine, the chestnut and the poppy. In the south of England the Romans developed vineyards to produce the wines with which they were familiar in their homeland.

Perhaps the most novel feature of Roman farming in Britain was the villas. These were large estates owned by rich Romans, and there were many throughout the Midlands and the south of England. The fields were cultivated by gangs of slaves, and in some villas a clothing factory had been installed.

The living quarters for the owners and their families in the villas were often quite luxurious. One of the best known was the villa at Chedworth in Gloucester, and it had over 20 rooms in three wings built round a courtyard. There was a private bath suite rather like modern Turkish baths, while most of the rooms had beautifully tessellated or mosaic marble floors and costly tapestries on the walls.

And yet for all the wealth and grandeur of the villas, the Romans did not really introduce any very revolutionary ideas of farming into Britain. Most of the country was still farmed by the Celts or Britons in their square fields and in the same old traditional ways. Thus, in the fifth century AD, when the Romans finally left Britain, the Britons were left to carry on almost as they had been doing before the Roman Conquest.

7 (*below*) Traces of a Romano-British village and fields in Cambridgeshire

8 (*opposite*) Aerial photograph of remains of the Roman villa at Chedworth. Note the evidence of the dwellings and buildings grouped round a courtyard. (The roofed buildings are modern)

The Anglo-Saxons

The Britons were not allowed to remain undisturbed for long, however, for about AD 450 Britain was invaded by the Anglo-Saxons from Germany. These peoples had been attacking the Roman Empire for many years, and now they began to settle in England in large numbers. They landed on the south and east coasts, and steadily the Britons were pushed back into Wales and Cornwall.

The Anglo-Saxon period (AD 450–1066) was an extremely important one in the development of English farming. Whereas the Britons and the Romans had in the main confined their farming to the lighter and drier upland districts, the Anglo-Saxons began to settle in and to farm the rich, heavy clay soils of the valleys. Much of England was covered with woods and forests when they arrived, and many of the river valleys were flooded, but over the centuries the Anglo-Saxon farmers cleared and drained the land.

By 1066, therefore, the character of the country had been completely changed, and most of the farming land in use today had been brought under cultivation. All this was a heroic achievement, and the generations of unknown Anglo-Saxon farmers who were responsible did more for the prosperity of England than many of the great heroes whose names feature so prominently in the history books.

The manner in which the Anglo-Saxons had settled in their new lands was also very important for the development of English agriculture. Normally when a small tribe or group of families took over a valley or district, the men would all join together in the work of clearing the land. They all helped to cut down the

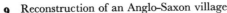

9 Reconstruction of an Anglo-Saxon village

trees, root out the stumps, and drain the land. Then when the land was cleared, each family would contribute an ox to make up the plough team. All the men helped in the ploughing, and then they would each receive a share of the available land. The individual farmer might sow and look after his plot by himself, but at harvest time they would all join together again to bring in the crops.

Gradually this pattern of co-operative farming became permanent. Many of the tasks like ploughing, harvesting and tending the livestock were carried out by groups of farmers working in common. Thus, where the Britons had each farmed their own individual small farm, now the Anglo-Saxons had grouped themselves into small villages or hamlets where a number of farmers and villagers worked together to cultivate the land.

In most instances, however, the lands of the village did not actually belong to the villagers. From the eighth century, many areas were open to attack from Viking raiders, and more and more villages began to look to some powerful chief or lord for protection. The ownership of the land was entrusted to him, and the villagers provided him with produce and labour. In return, the lord and his warriors took the villagers under his protection and defended them against their enemies.

In their farming practices the Anglo-Saxons concentrated on the growing of wheat, barley and oats. They had also large herds of sheep, cattle and pigs. Pigs were an especially important part of their agriculture, and some lords had as many as 2,000 pigs in their herds. The pigs in Anglo-Saxon times, however, were savage beasts and quite unlike the rather docile creatures of today. Often they grazed in a semi-wild condition in the woodland and forests, and pig hunting was a favourite sport with many Anglo-Saxons.

The Normans

The Anglo-Saxons, therefore, were highly successful farmers, and they did much to create a flourishing farming system in England. In 1066, however, their control over the country and over its agriculture came to an end when England was invaded by the Normans led by Duke William of Normandy. William the Conqueror, as he became known, had a certain claim to the English throne, and after he had defeated the English ruler, Harold Godwin, at Hastings, he was crowned king. He and his Norman followers then proceeded to take possession of England and all the lands throughout the country.

The Normans did not come in large numbers to dispossess the existing farmers as the Anglo-Saxons themselves had done six hundred years earlier. Instead they formed a small ruling class which seized the ownership of the various estates. The Anglo-Saxon lords were expelled from their lands, and new Norman lords were installed in their place. The English villagers and farmers continued much as before, but they now had a Norman lord who usually made much heavier demands on them. Indeed the Normans often looked upon the Saxon villagers as mere vassals or serfs. They therefore compelled them to work for many days each week on their lord's lands and to pay over livestock and produce as a kind of rental at regular intervals.

As William the Conqueror and his Norman lords settled in to take over and rule their new lands and possessions, they naturally wished to discover just how extensive and how valuable their estates and holdings actually were. In 1086, therefore, the King had a survey made of all the land in the kingdom. Commissioners were sent to every corner of England to examine and investigate each estate and farm. They measured the fields and woodland, they counted the numbers of pigs, sheep and cattle, they examined the fish and fishponds, they counted and listed the numbers of watermills and windmills, they found out how many ploughs and other implements there were, and carefully they ferreted out every last detail that might give useful information to the King. The results for every area of the kingdom were then written down in a great volume known as the *Domesday Book*.

The *Domesday Book* is an absolute mine of information about English farming in the eleventh century. It is from its pages that we can judge just how much the Anglo-Saxons had achieved, and we can also obtain a complete picture of the farms in every part of the country. Here, for example, is the report on Godman-chester in Huntingdonshire: 'There is land for 57 ploughs. There is a priest and a church; 3 mills rendering 100 shillings; 160 acres of meadow; and 50 acres of woodland.'

And so England found itself at the beginning of a new era in its farming history. The Anglo-Saxons had brought most of the country under cultivation, but now new owners were in control of the situation. The Normans were great organisers and administrators, and soon they had completed a pattern and a system of farming that was to endure for several centuries.

10 (*left*) Richmond Castle, Yorkshire. Built by Count Alan of Brittany, a follower of William the Conqueror, it has the typically Norman curtain wall and rectangular gatehouse

11 (*right*) Ploughing in the Middle Ages

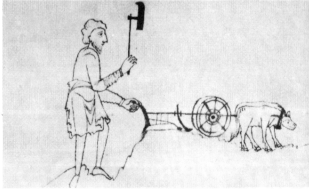

3 Farming in the Middle Ages

The Feudal System

After he had conquered England, William of Normandy became in theory the owner of all the lands in the country. He handed over large estates to his principal followers or barons, and in return they had to provide him with soldiers or perform certain services. The barons then gave out smaller estates to knights who would fight for the baron or the king when required. Many of the knights had possession of a manor or village, and from the labour and produce of the English villagers they maintained themselves and their families. Over the years this system, known as the feudal system, was consolidated in England, and the services which each man owed to his lord and superior became fixed by custom.

The Medieval Village

In large parts of England, particularly in the Midlands and the south, the basic unit of the feudal system was the village. Normally a village would form part of the estate of some lord who might have his manor house nearby. Round the lord's house was his park or private demesne. The village itself consisted of a few thatched huts, a church, a common or green, and perhaps an ale-house. Throughout the Middle Ages the majority of ordinary Englishmen lived and worked in such villages, and they followed a familiar and traditional way of life there.

The land belonging to the village was formed into two or three great open fields. The fields were divided into strips, and each villager had a certain number of strips scattered here and there throughout the fields. In addition there was also a large meadow and a common where the villagers could graze a fixed number of cows and sheep. They also had the right of grazing pigs in the waste land surrounding the village, and they could gather wood from the forests. Each house normally had a patch of land for growing vegetables and for the villagers' poultry.

In return for their lands, the villagers in medieval times performed certain services for their lords. Only a very few were freemen, and such fortunate men normally had about 30 acres of land. As rent for their holdings they gave the lord a proportion of their crops and sometimes an animal on special occasions.

Of the unfree villagers, the most numerous were the villeins. Some had as much land as the freemen, but they were tied to the village and could not leave without the lord's consent. They had to work two or three days each week on their lord's land, while at harvest time this duty might be extended to six days. They also had to hand over some eggs at Easter, a chicken at Christmas, and part of their crops in the autumn. Then when a villein died, his son and heir had to give the lord his

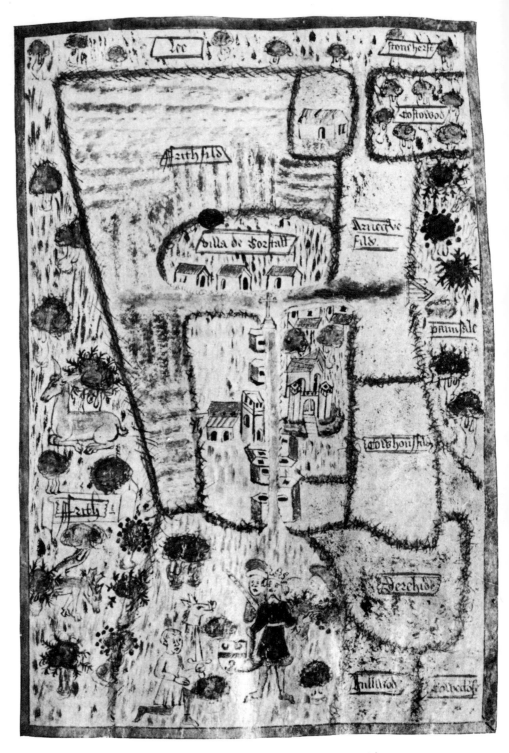

12 Village of Boarstall, Buckinghamshire, in the fifteenth century. After the Norman Conquest the lands there were given to Nigel, the huntsman, for slaying a boar in the Forest of Benwood

best beast in order to gain possession of his holdings.

Further down the scale were the cottars or bordars who might have only about 5 acres. Even more unfortunate were the serfs or bondsmen who had no land of their own at all. To earn a living, the serfs worked for the lord and the other villagers on their strips, and they would receive some food for their labours.

Medieval Farming

Over the years the methods and routine of farming in the medieval village became quite fixed, and the work throughout the various seasons followed a regular pattern. Thus in the early spring the villagers were busy ploughing their strips. A team of eight or twelve oxen was required to pull the heavy plough with its iron coulter, and each man brought one or two animals to make up the team. The plough was difficult to handle, and the furrows were rarely straight.

Only two out of the three great open fields were ploughed each year, for the medieval villagers practised a rotation of crops. The normal rotation was wheat or rye in the first year, barley or oats in the second, and in the third year the field lay fallow. This rotation was repeated year after year, and thus in any one year a third of the land lay fallow so that it could recover from the previous two years' crops. Animals grazed in the fallow field, and their manure helped to make it more fertile again.

After the fields had been ploughed, the villagers would sow seed on their strips. Oats and barley were sown in the spring, and wheat was planted in late autumn. The seed was not sown in drills, but was scattered broadcast. The villager slung a basket round his neck and threw the seed to either side of him as he walked up and down his strip. This method of sowing was not very efficient, and produced a rather low yield. It also made weeding a very tiresome task, for there were no neat regular rows for hoeing as in later times.

Summer brought sheep-shearing and haymaking, but the busiest time of the year was the autumn when the crops were harvested. The villagers worked in teams of five, four cutting and one binding. The oats, rye and barley were cut with scythes, but for wheat sickles were used. Then when all this heavy work was completed, there was great rejoicing, and there would be a great harvest-home celebration. There was feasting and drinking, sports were held on the village green, and there was singing and dancing in the evenings.

After the festivities, the villagers resumed their labours. The corn was now threshed by hand with a flail made of two pieces of wood tied together by a leather thong. One end was brought down on the ears of corn to force out the grain. The chaff was blown away with a large fan, and then the women scooped up the grain into sacks in readiness for transporting to the mill. Some of the villagers ground their own corn into flour with hand mills or rotary querns, but if they were discovered they would be fined. The lord insisted that all corn must be taken to the mill and that a proportion of the flour should be set aside for him.

The mill normally stood by a stream and was driven by water power, but in

some villages there might be a windmill. The miller took a percentage of the grain for himself as well as for the lord, but most villagers suspected him of taking more than his fair share. He had such a reputation for dishonesty that the answer expected in the popular medieval riddle: 'What is the boldest thing in the world?' was: 'A miller's shirt, for it clasps a thief daily by the throat'.

After the ploughing and sowing of the winter crop, the villagers began preparing for winter. Wild fruits and berries were gathered, while bracken was cut to serve as bedding for the cattle. Logs were cut, and a large wood-pile was built up outside each house. Every man would also make sure that his house was water-proof, and often he would thatch his roof or re-cover the walls with clay or mud.

Sometime in November, too, most of the animals were killed off and the meat salted. There were no crops such as turnips to provide winter feed, and thus only a small number of animals could be kept alive through the winter. These were fed on hay and straw, but often some of them starved to death. Then a few of the wretched beasts which survived might die through eating too greedily when they were taken from their stalls in the spring. As an old rhyme tells us:

> From Christmas to May
> Weak cattle decay;
> When grass doth appear
> Worst danger is near.

This general pattern of farming followed by the medieval villagers throughout the year helped to make each village almost self-supporting. The villagers produced all their own food, made their own clothes from the wool taken from their sheep, built their own huts and houses, and constructed their simple furniture

13 (*opposite*) Open fields at Laxton in Nottinghamshire
14 Ploughing and sowing seed broadcast in the fourteenth century

and bedding. The only articles which they obtained from outside the village were the stones for the mill, the iron for the ploughs and other implements, and the salt used to preserve meat. In the main, too, they did not grow crops or rear animals to sell them for a profit like a modern farmer, for there were only small towns and no great outside demand for food supplies.

To some modern people this whole system of farming in medieval times might seem very inefficient. The villagers wasted a great deal of time moving from one strip to another, and much of the land was wasted in the balks that separated one strip from another. The fallow field, too, was wasteful of land, for each year a third of the land was left uncultivated.

15 Digging an irrigation ditch in the thirteenth century. There is some sort of pumping system on the right, behind the man who seems to be the 'foreman'

The medieval system of farming was also inefficient in that it prevented the individual farmer from improving his holding. If a man had a lazy neighbour, then weeds would blow across on to his strips. With the animals all grazing together on the common, moreover, any disease would spread like wildfire through the herds. It was also impossible to improve the livestock by selective breeding, and the general standards of the cattle and sheep tended to remain low.

And yet it would be quite wrong and unfair if we were to become too critical of the medieval farmers. Year after year and century after century they followed their rotations and produced regular harvests to feed a population that was growing steadily larger. They also maintained and even increased the fertility of the soil, and made their holdings more productive. All in all this was a wonderful achievement, and later generations have benefited from the care and devotion with which they tended their lands.

The people of medieval times of course were much more closely linked with the land and the countryside than the inhabitants of our modern towns and cities. Their whole lives were in a sense wrapped up in their work and farming. Their festivals and holidays, for instance, were mostly all connected with the working year, while their methods of measuring and counting were derived from farming activities. The acre and furlong were measurements associated with the area and

16 Beekeeping was an important aspect of medieval farming as honey was used as a sweetener until replaced by imported sugar. Many monasteries had a large apiary

length of a strip, while the length of a cricket field was based on the width of a normal strip.

In the way the people all helped each other, too, the medieval system of farming was very different from that of modern times. Thus where most modern farmers have their own separate holdings and farms, the medieval villager lived and worked in a close and co-operative community. The rights of the community were more important than those of the individual, and no one was allowed to do anything which might affect the interests of others. Perhaps the ambitious and efficient farmer was held back, but at least no one could carry on any activity that might have a harmful effect on the interests and holdings of others.

Wales, Ireland and Scotland

Hitherto in this chapter we have been describing the open field system of farming which was practised throughout much of England during the Middle Ages, but there were many parts of the British Isles where this system was not adopted. In the west country and Wales, for example, the square fields of Celtic times still survived. Most of the farmers of Wales indeed lived as shepherds or herders moving around from pasture to pasture with their flocks. Huge estates were owned by the Welsh princes, and the smaller farmers and herders paid them a rental of money and food. After Wales was conquered by Edward I in the thirteenth century, however, the English system was introduced into the Vale of Glamorgan, Pembroke and a few other places, but in most areas sheep farming continued to be the normal pattern of farming.

In Ireland, too, most of the farmers were shepherds or herders, and many of them led a wandering life moving from pasture to pasture. On the east coast round Dublin, however, an area that had been conquered and settled by the Normans, a type of farming similar to that in England was carried on. Villages like those in England were established, and the native Irish became villeins and serfs working for their conquerors. But the open field system never became as firmly established in Ireland as in England.

Scotland was of course a quite separate country in this period, and in the Lowlands there developed a different pattern of farming known as the infield-outfield system. The infield consisted of irregularly shaped patches of ploughed land lying close to a hamlet or settlement. These fields received all the manure that was available, and oats and barley were grown on them year after year. When the soil was completely exhausted the patches would be left fallow and others brought into cultivation.

Further away from the hamlet were the outfields. These were patches of poorer lands, and here too oats and barley were cultivated till the soil was exhausted. It was then allowed to rest for four or five years while other patches were ploughed and cultivated.

In Scotland there were few real villages as in England, and the normal unit was a toun or hamlet. This consisted of a cluster of six or eight huts occupied by a group of families working their lands in common. As in England the various fields were divided into strips, known in Scotland as rigs. There was rarely a meadow or common in a Scottish toun, and cattle and sheep were grazed on rough pastureland or on the outfields when these were not being cultivated.

In the hilly and mountainous parts of Scotland, however, there was little arable farming. In the Borders, for example, sheep farming was the main occupation of the people. The abbeys and churches owned much of the land in this area, and in the thirteenth century Kelso Abbey had as many as 7,000 sheep on its estates. In the Highlands the clansmen concentrated mainly on rearing cattle. These were the ancestors of the modern Highland cattle, and were of a reddish brown colour. The Highlanders grazed their cattle in low-lying valleys and glens in spring and winter, while in the summer months the cattle were taken to shielings or grazing lands high in the hills.

17 Peasants killing pigs in the fourteenth century

4   Progress and Advances

The medieval system of farming that we have been studying continued for several centuries with relatively little change, but as time went on certain modifications appeared. In the first place trade increased and towns steadily grew in number and size during the thirteenth and fourteenth centuries, and thus there was much more opportunity for bondsmen and unfree farmers to flee to the towns and find employment there. If they remained at liberty for a year and a day, then they became freemen and could not be taken back to their villages.

With the growth of towns, too, there was a greater demand for food. Villagers were thus encouraged to produce a little more than they themselves required so that they could sell some of their crops in the neighbouring towns. They obtained money for their produce, and this enabled many of them to buy their freedom or to replace their labour services to the lord with a money rent. Many of the lords were short of funds and desperately eager to get their hands on ready cash, especially in the period of the Crusades when they found it extremely expensive to equip an expedition to the Holy Land.

The great series of plagues which swept through England and Europe in the fourteenth century also helped to bring about changes in agriculture. These culminated in the Black Death of 1349–51 which killed off between a third and a half of all the villagers in England. With these terrible casualties, many holdings were left untended, and there was a serious shortage of labour. The lords were therefore ready to grant improved conditions, and thus again many villagers obtained their freedom and the removal of burdensome duties.

The Wool Trade: Sheep Farming

The growth of the wool trade in the later Middle Ages also helped to bring about changes in the medieval system of farming. England produced the best wool in Europe at this time, and by the fourteenth century Flemish and Italian clothing manufacturers were ready to buy as much English wool as they could obtain. The price of wool rose sharply, and many lords, realising that it was more profitable to rear sheep than to grow wheat and barley, turned their lands into sheep runs. Some were not content with this, however, and during the fifteenth century they began to take over the commons and to build walls or hedges round them.

Some of the finest and most valuable wool in England came from a short-woolled breed of sheep that grazed on the upland pastures of the West Midlands, Herefordshire and Shropshire. The fleece from this sheep produced a thinner fibre than any other animal in Europe save the Spanish Merino. Leominster was the centre of the trade in this fine wool, and writers in the sixteenth century called it Lemster Ore. The old medieval Leicester sheep also produced good wool, and their fleece was said to be unequalled in Europe for fineness and strength.

The development of the wool trade brought considerable prosperity to many ordinary Englishmen during the fifteenth century. Large numbers of small farmers had gained possession of their own lands and holdings, and they were able to make good profits from sheep farming. Prices were rising rapidly towards the end of the century, moreover, and since their rentals were fixed and were not increased, their position was greatly improved. Some were able to rent extra areas of land and to become substantial farmers. This new prospering group came to be known as the yeomen, and they were among the most important class in England in the sixteenth century under the Tudors.

The Tudors

The accession of the Tudors to the English throne in 1485 also brought certain benefits to English farming. The Wars of the Roses had disrupted the life of many areas of the country, but now there were more settled and peaceful conditions. This enabled the yeomen and other farmers to flourish and prosper still further,

18   A shepherd from Edmund Spencer's *Shepherd's Calendar* (1579)

and steadily the wealth of the country was increased as the wool trade expanded.

Under Henry VIII a new development occurred when the monasteries were dissolved in 1536 and 1539 at the time of the Reformation. The monasteries had for long possessed large estates and some of the best land in the country, and now this was distributed amongst the King's supporters. A large amount of the monastic lands eventually fell into the hands of the yeomen or of rich merchants who had decided to move out from the towns, and they frequently turned it into sheep farms.

The change over to sheep farming in many districts of England during the fifteenth and sixteenth centuries certainly brought prosperity to many yeomen and other farmers, but for large numbers of villagers and small farmers it caused considerable suffering and distress. With several lords enclosing the commons, the villagers lost their grazing rights, and many could no longer make a living from their strips. They were therefore forced to sell their strips to the landlord or to some richer neighbour. In some districts, too, the lord was able to persuade or to compel the villagers to give up their strips in the open fields, and these were then enclosed as sheep runs.

Normally those villagers who had sold or had been forced out of their land tried to obtain employment working for the lord or for their wealthier neighbours. But sheep farming required only a few workers, and thus only a few could find

19 (*opposite*) Longleat House, Wiltshire, built between 1550 and 1580. This house is a fine example of Elizabethan architecture and takes its name from the *long leat*, or stream, which fed a mill near this spot in medieval times. A small Augustinian priory had occupied this site from about 1270, but was dissolved in the reign of Henry VIII. The property then passed through the hands of several eminent men to John Thynne, a protégé of the Lord Protector Somerset. His marriage to the daughter of a wealthy merchant helped him to buy more land and later he began building the house

20 A Tudor timbered farm house. The outside staircase suggests that maybe only the top floor was used for living quarters. Perhaps the ground floor was for animals or, from the width of the gate, for carts

employment there. Many villagers, therefore, left their homes to seek work in neighbouring towns or took to the road as beggars or vagabonds. Whole villages were deserted, and as Sir Thomas More, a famous sixteenth-century writer, observed, the sheep 'that were wont to be so myke and tame and so smal eaters, now be become so great devourers that they eate up and swallow down the very men themselves'.

The large numbers of people forced to leave their homes and taking to the roads as beggars and vagabonds were a serious problem to the government in Tudor times. Many moved from village to village and from house to house pestering, tricking and threatening the inhabitants. Some tried to win sympathy and money by covering their limbs with sores or by placing soap in their mouth and pretending they had the falling sickness (epilepsy).

When they could not obtain money by begging, many vagabonds began to steal. Some known as 'Anglers' used long poles to 'fish' clothes from hedges, while others called 'Riggers' stole horses from fields. Sometimes whole gangs of these ruffians would work together under a leader called the Upright Man. Normally he was a fierce, violent fellow, and he collected a portion of all the money taken or stolen by the members of the gang.

The government was exceedingly alarmed by all these disorders, and it passed several Acts including the Poor Law of 1601 in an attempt to stamp them out. Any able-bodied person over fourteen convicted of begging was to be 'grievously whipped and burnt through the gristle of the right ear with a hot iron of the compass of an inch about'. If this did not deter a man from begging and he was

21 A group of vagabonds being driven through the streets in the sixteenth century

convicted a third time, then he could be sentenced to death. Large numbers of beggars were also rounded up by the authorities and forced to clean out the filthy ditches around London and other cities. This latter treatment seems to have had some effect, for, as one judge wrote, the vagabonds would rather 'hazard their lives than work'.

The sufferings of the dispossessed villagers and the vagabonds in Tudor England contrasted sharply with the growing wealth and prosperity of the yeomen and the upper classes. This wealth was soon displayed in large-scale improvements to the farms and houses. Thus instead of the draughty thatched-roof house of medieval times, the yeomen farmers began to build the typical Tudor half-timbered and plastered house for themselves. Glazed windows and chimneys were installed, while featherbeds and other new articles of furniture were purchased to make their homes more comfortable.

Even more impressive were the mansions or 'palaces' built by the great lords who had made fortunes from sheep farming or the dissolution of the monasteries. Some of these were three-storey buildings with fanciful turrets and battlements. They had great oriel windows, and all the stonework was decorated with tracery and carvings. Normally they were surrounded with magnificent terraces and beautifully laid-out gardens. All in all these great houses and the homes of the yeomen helped give the English countryside a much pleasanter and more prosperous appearance.

22 Outlines of a medieval village in Lincolnshire, deserted in Tudor times

Improvements in Farming

In addition to the development of sheep farming in this period, several important agricultural developments and improvements were also taking place. Since many farmers now had enclosed farms, they also had the opportunity to experiment without the interference of other strip holders as in a medieval village. Thus throughout the late sixteenth century and the seventeenth century, many new farming techniques and implements were introduced. The Civil War in the 1640s disrupted activities in several areas, but it did not halt the steady improvement in the conditions of English farming.

Some of the improvements taking place can be seen in the writings of the Elizabethan agriculturalist, Thomas Tusser (c. 1573). Thus he mentions new rotations of crops, and his four-course rotation of barley, pulse, wheat and fallow was a distinct advance on medieval practices. Tucker also mentions developments in manuring the fields, and he indicates that improved types of spades, scythes and other implements were being used.

Several new crops such as clover and hops were also being cultivated towards the end of the sixteenth century. Marling was being used as a fertiliser, and it considerably increased the yields obtained. Marl is a mixture of clay and lime, and it was particularly valuable as a manure for light soils.

Many landowners and yeoman farmers also made strenuous efforts to bring new land into cultivation by draining marshes and swamps. The most ambitious attempts were made by a goup of landlords who tried to drain the Fens in the seventeenth century. They employed a Dutch engineer named Vermuyden, and he was able to reclaim thousands of acres. His work, however, encountered bitter resistance from the fenmen when they realised that the draining of the land would drive off the wild fowl upon which they depended for a living. Their feelings were described by a local poet who declared:

> The feathered fowls have wings to fly to other nations,
> But we have no such things to help our transportations;
> We must give place (oh grievous case!) to horned beasts and cattle,
> Except that we can all agree to drive them out by battle!

And by battle the fenmen certainly did attempt to defend their old way of life. Moving by night along secret paths known only to themselves, they broke down the newly built banks and pushed the unfortunate engineers into the treacherous waters of the fens where they drowned without trace. Not surprisingly the work of draining the Fens was delayed, and it was not completed successfully until modern times when it has become one of the richest agricultural areas in the country.

Important as all these developments were, however, we must not exaggerate the extent of the changes that were affecting English farming during the sixteenth and seventeenth centuries. Certainly there were enclosures in many areas, but the open field system survived throughout the greater part of the country. Nevertheless, even in those districts which had retained the open field system, some progress was being made. Throughout the seventeenth century, for instance, more and more farmers were changing over from growing rye to wheat. Again, potatoes had been brought from the New World at the end of the sixteenth century, and though they were not yet generally regarded as a crop suitable for growing in fields, they were being cultivated in gardens. Other vegetables that were being grown increasingly in villagers' gardens at this time were turnips, cabbages, carrots and celery.

23 A page from a tract on husbandry written in 1592

¶Here followe certayne wayes of plan-
ting and graffing, with other neceſſaries herein mete
to be knowne, tranſlated out of Dutche by.L.M.

¶ To graffe one Vine on another.

Ou that will graffe one vyne vpon another , ye ſhall (in Januarp) cleaue the head of the vine, as ye do other ſtockes, and then put in pour Uine graffe or cyon , but firſt ye muſt pare him thin ,ere ye ſet him in the head, then clap and moſſe him as the other .

¶.Choſen dayes to graffe in, and to chofe your cions.

ALſo when ſo euer that ye will graffe, the beſt choſen times is on the laſt day before the chaunge, and alſo in the chaunge,and on the ſecond day after the chaunge, if ye graffe(as ſome ſay)on the thirde, fourth ę fyft day after the chaunge,

24 An illustration from a Tudor book on farming, Fitzherbert's *Husbandrye* (1525)

5   The Agricultural Revolution

We have seen that though certain changes and improvements had taken place in English farming during the fifteenth, sixteenth and seventeenth centuries, yet the open field system still survived practically unaltered in many parts of the country. When in the eighteenth century, however, Britain began to experience the full effects of the Industrial Revolution and a considerable rise in population, the weaknesses of the older type of farming became increasingly apparent. The swollen populations of the new factory towns required ever larger supplies of bread and meat, but the open field system was wasteful and inefficient and incapable of meeting the increased demand.

As extra demands were made on British farming and farmers, therefore, a new movement for the reform and improvement of our system of agriculture gained momentum. Thus in the eighteenth and early nineteenth centuries more and more of the land came to be enclosed into consolidated farms which could be worked more efficiently and which could be made to produce more food. Sometimes all the people in a village would see the need and would agree to a change, but in most places in England some villagers were always opposed to the idea and a special procedure was therefore necessary. If a majority of the farmers in a particular area desired enclosure, then they petitioned Parliament, and an Act would be passed authorising the enclosure of the villagers' lands.

After an Enclosure Act had been passed, commissioners were appointed to assess the amount of land each man had possessed under the old system and to allocate him an appropriate area of land in a consolidated holding. Between 1750 and 1850 about $5\frac{1}{2}$ million acres of lands were enclosed by Acts of Parliament, and by the latter date the open field system had practically disappeared. The countryside took on its modern pattern of a patchwork of fields, each surrounded by hedges or fences.

On the newly enclosed farms, as well as on those which had been enclosed in earlier centuries, farmers now had the opportunity of trying out new methods to increase the output of their lands. Many people were much more inclined to experiment in this period, for the scientific revolution of the seventeenth century had ushered in new scientific attitudes and a desire to discover more and more about the laws of nature. The first signs of these new attitudes in agriculture were the setting up of Botanical Gardens, where experiments were carried out to find the best ways of growing and improving various plants. Philosophical Societies were also founded in some districts, and these helped to spread the new ideas and findings that were being discovered in the experiments in the Botanical Gardens and elsewhere.

Stock-breeding

The new attitudes also affected the rearing and breeding of animals, and now that many farmers had complete control over their herds on enclosed farms, they could easily carry out experiments in improving their livestock. One of the many men who became interested in this aspect of farming was Robert Bakewell, a farmer born in Leicestershire in 1726. He travelled through Europe and purchased the best specimens of sheep he could find. Then by careful breeding of these animals with his own flocks he was able to produce the New Leicester, a type of sheep famous for the quantity and quality of its mutton.

While Bakewell was experimenting with sheep, other farmers were trying to improve their herds of cattle. Particularly prominent were the brothers, Charles and Robert Colling, who produced an improved breed of shorthorn on their farms near Darlington. Other famous eighteenth-century stockbreeders were the Davy family who developed the Devons, and Benjamin Tomkins who bred Herefords. In the early nineteenth century a further advance was made when Hugh Watson and William McCombie in Scotland produced the world famous Aberdeen-Angus breed of cattle.

25 A longhorn 'Brindled Beauty' bred by Robert Fowler

The story of how Watson and McCombie developed this famous breed is well worth telling as an illustration of the work of all these pioneers of stockbreeding in this country. It began in 1810 when Hugh Watson went to market at Brechin and purchased ten heifers and a bull. By skilful breeding he soon produced an excellent animal, and in 1829 he won prizes at the Smithfield Show.

William McCombie was extremely impressed by Watson's achievements, and he decided to carry on his work at his own farm in Aberdeenshire. In 1867 his steer, 'Black Prince', created such a sensation that Queen Victoria had it taken to the royal farm at Windsor so that she might inspect it. Then in 1878, at the International Show at Paris, McCombie won the special prize awarded to the exhibitor of the best group of animals for beef-producing purposes in the entire Exhibition. From that time the Aberdeen-Angus has been ranked as one of the world's best breeds of beef cattle.

The successes achieved by such stockbreeders as Watson and McCombie, Bakewell and the Collings brothers did much to improve Britain's food supply. Much more meat was now obtained from cattle and sheep, and the quality was

26 Robert Bakewell hiring out his rams to other farmers. In this way the New Leicester breed of sheep was spread quickly throughout the country

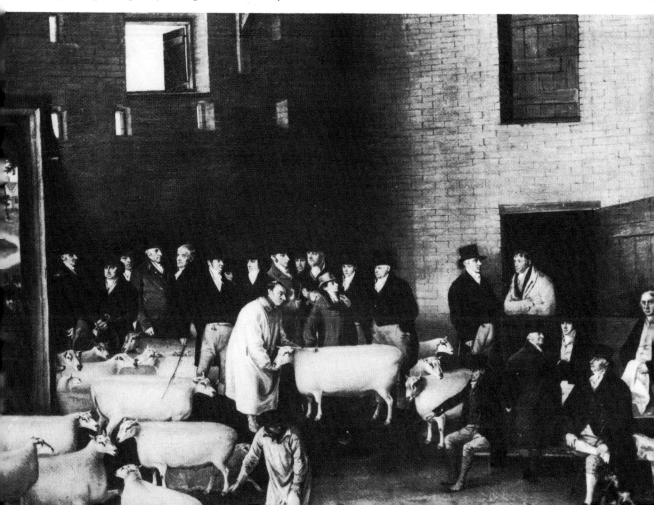

incomparably better. In the years between 1710 and 1795, for example, the average weight of cattle and sheep sold at Smithfield market in London more than doubled. Dairy cows, too, were improved, and such breeds as the Ayrshire produced large quantities of milk.

New Crops and Rotations

Another important advance in agriculture in the eighteenth century was the introduction of new crops such as turnips. This plant had been grown in gardens before this time and even in fields by a few farmers in the seventeenth century, but it was not until after 1736 when Lord Townshend began growing turnips on his farm in Norfolk that its use as a field crop became widespread.

Lord Townshend also introduced a four course rotation—the famous Norfolk rotation of turnips, barley, grass and clover, and wheat. This rotation ended the necessity for leaving a third of the land fallow each year, while the turnips provided winter feed for the livestock. Farmers could therefore keep more animals, and these in turn provided more manure to improve the fertility of their fields.

Townshend's rotation was soon being adopted in many areas, and its popularity is illustrated by the following story concerning an English rector. About 1770, it seems, the rector was visited by his archdeacon, who was shocked to find turnips

27 The Colling brothers, Charles and Robert

being grown in the churchyard. 'This must not happen again', he declared sternly, pointing to the turnips. 'Oh no, sir', replied the rector innocently. 'Next year it will be barley!'

New Seeds

As well as experimenting with new crops and rotations, British farmers at this time also sought to improve the quality of their grain seeds. The methods they adopted at first, however, were often haphazard, and such improvements as they achieved frequently came about by accident or as the result of intelligent observation. One of the most famous of the early improved barley seeds, for example, the Chevallier barley, was discovered in 1820 by a Suffolk farm labourer named John Andrews. One evening he noticed an ear of barley in his boot which seemed better than the ordinary seeds. He kept it and sowed it the following spring, and it produced excellent grain. A clergyman, the Rev. John Chevallier, heard of what he had done, and he planted some of the seed in his fields. The new seed proved to be a much better yielding variety than the ordinary seeds, and it very quickly passed into general use. Unfortunately the people of the time did not think a mere labourer worthy of recognition, and so the seed was named after the clergyman and not after John Andrews.

28 *The Reapers*, painted by George Stubbs, a famous artist of the late eighteenth century

As time went on, however, farmers became much more systematic in their attempts to obtain better yielding seeds. One of the men who perfectly illustrated this new approach was an American, Mark Carleton. After graduating in 1887 from Kansas Agricultural College, Carleton devoted his life to trying to discover a type of wheat which would be immune to disease and which could withstand severe winters. He first of all wrote to farmers in all parts of the world asking for samples of their seeds, and soon he had many thousands of different varieties. Then he sowed the seeds in separate little plots and compared their yields and performance.

At last, after many years of experimenting, Carleton found a variety of Russian wheat known as Kubanka wheat which seemed to have all the qualities he desired. He obtained large supplies of it and persuaded many American farmers to grow it. His faith in Kubanka wheat was soon shown to have been well founded, for it produced excellent crops, and in 1904 it proved itself to be immune to the dreaded

29 Jethro Tull's seed drill

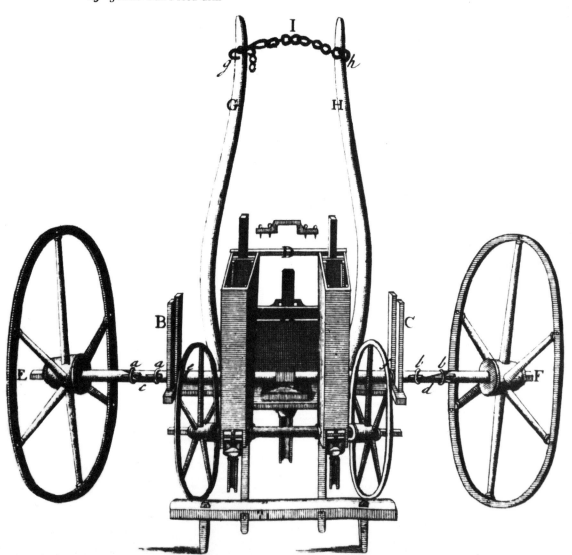

black stem rust which ravaged the fields of Kansas in that year and destroyed all the other varieties of wheat. A few years later Carleton obtained another type of wheat from Russia known as Kharkov wheat. This, too, proved to be ideally suited to American conditions, and together with Kubanka wheat it vastly increased the output of the American prairie farms.

In modern times, of course, the type of work undertaken by Carleton is now carried on in Agricultural Colleges and in Research Institutes by teams of scientists and experts. Continually they are experimenting with seeds and trying to produce even better varieties by crossing one seed with another. Their work, like that of the early pioneers, is of great benefit to the ordinary farmer and to the whole of mankind.

Mechanisation

Another significant development in British agriculture beginning in the eighteenth century was the introduction of new farming machines. In earlier centuries many men had tried to invent machines to perform certain farming operations, but the first really practical one was the drill for sowing seed invented by Jethro Tull, an Oxfordshire farmer, in 1701. This machine set seeds in a straight drill at regular intervals and then covered them over with earth. Tull also invented a horse-drawn hoe for weeding between the rows of seed. His inventions proved very successful, for he was able to sow his fields with only a quarter of the seed required by the old method of sowing broadcast, while his yields per acre were about three times as large as formerly.

Tull's machine, however, was merely the forerunner of a large number of new mechanical inventions which have over the years transformed the practice of farming. Towards the end of the eighteenth century, for instance, men became interested in inventing a mechanical reaper. One of the best attempts to invent

30 Robert McCormick's reaping machine

such a machine was made by a Scottish farmer, Patrick Bell, about 1826; but since no one in Britain seemed very interested in his ideas he abandoned his efforts. It was an American named Robert McCormick who produced the first successful reaper, and later McCormick invented a combine-harvester which reaped and threshed at the same time.

While McCormick was successfully developing his reaping machine, other inventors in the nineteenth century were trying to produce a steam tractor to pull a plough. None of these was really successful, however, for the machines were so heavy that they tended to sink deep down into the earth. Later a steam engine was invented which remained standing at the edge of a field and hauled the plough backwards and forwards by means of wire ropes. But it was not till the development of the internal combustion engine and the invention of the tractor that a really effective substitute for the horse was discovered. The tractor has, of course, revolutionised modern farming, and today it is the principal means of operating the ever increasing number of machines that are being invented to help our farmers.

Propagating the New Ideas

Important as were the achievements of such farmers as Bakewell, Lord Townshend and Jethro Tull, the new methods of farming which they developed might not have had very much influence if it had not been for the work of a small number of men who saw to it that the new ideas were made known to almost all the farmers in the country. One of these men was Thomas Coke, a large landowner in Norfolk. His estate was in a poor condition when he inherited it in 1776, but he quickly learned of the new methods and began to make improvements. He introduced better breeds of sheep, marled and manured his lands, and held annual sheep-shearing festivals to which farmers and breeders came from all over the country.

31 Arthur Young, Secretary of the Board of Agriculture

44

At these festivals farmers were able to exchange ideas and to find out about all the latest developments that were taking place. In a sense these festivals of Coke's were the forerunners of the later Agricultural Shows which have done so much for British farming.

Another man who did much to publicise the new farming techniques was Arthur Young, a prominent eighteenth-century writer. He travelled round the countryside and then wrote books telling of what he had witnessed on his travels. Later, in 1793, he became Secretary of the newly established Board of Agriculture, and under his direction the Board produced a stream of reports which provided a great deal of information and advice for farmers.

Even more influential, perhaps, than either Coke or Young in making the new methods of farming popular was the King, George III (1760–1820). He had a model farm at Windsor, and so enthusiastic was he about this farm and about farming in general that he became known as 'Farmer George'. He was interested in livestock breeding, and imported Merino sheep from Spain in 1792. He also wrote articles under the pen name of Ralph Robinson in a farming magazine published by Arthur Young. Naturally, the fact that the King himself was interested in the new farming methods encouraged many farmers to follow his example and to adopt them.

32 King George III rewards an industrious haymaker near Weymouth

6   The New Farming

The Agrarian Revolution beginning in the eighteenth century brought about tremendous changes in the whole way of life in Britain. Together with the Industrial Revolution taking place about the same time, it transformed the country from a largely rural society where the great majority of people were farmers to one of large towns and cities with an increasing number of people working in factories. As the enclosures and the new methods of farming were introduced, so large numbers of people left the country districts and moved to the towns to swell the populations there. Over the years this process has been intensified, and steadily the percentage of the people engaged in farming has declined. Today after two hundred years of change and transformation of the countryside we are left with a mere 3 per cent of the population in agricultural employment in Britain, and the vast majority of the people live in towns and work in industry or commerce.

The Agrarian Revolution also introduced important changes within the world of agriculture itself, and the organisation of farming in late eighteenth-century England was completely altered. Thus, where small communities of villagers holding land from their lord and working their fields had been the norm in medieval England, now a new pattern appeared. Normally the land was still owned by a landlord or squire, but he rented it out in enclosed and consolidated farms and holdings to substantial tenants. These tenants were often those villagers who had somehow been able to find the money for the enclosures and who had taken over the holdings of their less fortunate neighbours. The tenant farmers in turn employed farm labourers to work their enlarged holdings, and paid them a small wage in money and in produce. These labourers were usually villagers who had been forced to sell their own holdings.

Many of the tenant farmers quickly discovered that they could become quite prosperous by adopting the new rotations and the new methods of farming. Britain was involved in many wars in the late eighteenth century, and the restriction of foreign imports kept the price of grain high. The rapidly growing populations of the towns, too, provided an increasing demand for food, and provided ready markets for the increased crops they were able to turn out from their fields. Many farmers indeed became quite wealthy, and throughout the agricultural districts of England and Scotland substantial and prosperous houses and steadings appeared in the late eighteenth and early nineteenth centuries.

Despite the prosperous conditions, however, the tenant farmers were also faced with many novel and perplexing problems. In the first place, they now found that their success and fortune had come to depend on something they themselves could not control, namely the prices they were able to obtain for their produce in the market. In earlier times the main concern for the vast majority of farmers had been to produce enough food for themselves and their families, but now practically all farmers were growing enough crops to sell and to make profits. Certainly they could earn substantial sums of money in good years, but at other times the prices slumped and they might find they were working at a loss.

Farmers soon discovered, too, that it was difficult to judge in advance what kind of prices they would obtain for their crops. A farmer, for instance, might look at his ripening fields and be certain of a good harvest, but if there was a bumper crop all over the country, then the price would be low and he would not receive as much money as he had expected. If, however, there was a poor harvest throughout Britain and a scarcity of grain, then prices would be high, but in this case the farmer might have only a poor crop to sell.

33 A prosperous farmer and his family

DRAINING.

Fig. 1.

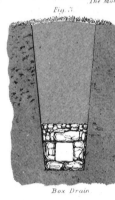

The Mole Drain Plough.

Fig. 2.   *Fig. 3.*   *Fig. 4.*   *Fig. 5.*

Wedge Drain.   *Box Drain.*   *Rubble Drain.*   *Horse shoe Tile Drain.*

Fig. 6.   *Fig. 7.*   *Fig. 8.*   *Fig. 9.*   *Fig. 10.*

Horse shoe Tile and Sole.

Fig. 11.

Pipe Drain.   *Pipe with Collar.*   *Double Tile Main Drain.*   *Triple Tile Main Drain.*

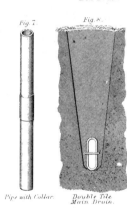

Spring Drain.

Fig. 12.   *Fig. 13.*   *Fig. 14.*   *Fig. 15.*   *Fig. 16.*   *Fig. 17.*

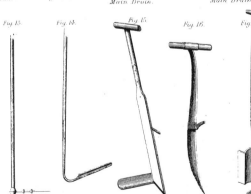

Implements suited for making various kinds of Drains.

Fig. 18.

Hand made Drain Tiles and Bricks.

The Corn Laws

Such difficulties were not, however, immediately apparent to farmers in the early days of the Agrarian Revolution. Throughout the long war with France and Napoleon, from 1793–1815, imports of foreign grain were severely cut, and British farmers could sell as much corn as they could produce at high prices. But with the ending of the war in 1815 the situation was drastically altered. Foreign corn could once more be imported in large quantities, and the competition from this source threatened to cause a slump in prices.

British farmers, therefore, began to demand that the import of foreign corn should be prohibited or severely restricted. Fortunately for them Parliament at this time was dominated by landlords who wished to see the farmers prosperous so that they could afford to pay high rents. Accordingly, in 1815 Parliament passed the Corn Laws which stated that no foreign corn should be imported into this country until British corn had reached the price of £4 a quarter.

Despite this measure, however, the years after 1815 were difficult ones for British agriculture. There was a general post-war depression in trade and industry, and farming prices fell to a low level. The Corn Laws did afford some protection to British farmers, but nevertheless many of them had to struggle hard to survive during the 1820s and 1830s.

The Golden Age

Towards the end of the 1830s, however, agriculture recovered and prosperity returned to Britain's farms. Farming in this country now entered the period which is often referred to as its 'Golden Age', a period which continued right down to the middle of the 1870s. There was an increasing demand for food, and the new railways enabled farmers to transport their produce cheaply and swiftly to the markets in the towns. They began once more to make large profits, and with these profits they made improvements on their farms. They bought new machinery and they drained their fields with the new clay pipes invented in 1843 by a certain John Reade. They began to apply artifical manures like nitrate of soda to their lands, and they purchased the new cattle cakes made from cotton seed, linseed and other materials to improve the feeding of their herds.

Beneath the surface of this glowing prosperity, however, forces were at work which were in the long run to undermine the position of British agriculture. An increasing number of people were being employed in the new factories, and since these factory workers were poorly paid, they wanted cheap food. If foreign corn was cheaper than British corn, then they saw no reason why they should be forced to pay more for a British loaf. The factory owners, too, wished for cheaper corn, for if the price of bread was low, then they would be able to keep their workers' wages at a low level. They also hoped that foreign countries would buy the goods produced in our factories if we imported corn from their farms.

Throughout the 1820s, 30s and 40s, as the power of the manufacturers increased, there was a growing demand for the repeal of the Corn Laws. In 1838 an Anti-Corn

49

34 (*opposite*) Field drainage: types of drains and equipment for making them

Law League was founded by Richard Cobden and John Bright. They were both fine speakers and they mounted a most impressive propaganda campaign which won them many supporters. They won over many MPs to their cause, but not enough to have the Corn Laws repealed.

Then, in 1845 the rains came and 'washed away the Corn Laws'. The harvest in England that year was a poor one, but worse still the Irish potato crop failed, and thousands upon thousands of people died of starvation. The arguments for allowing the import of foreign corn to feed the hungry millions now seemed overwhelming, and in 1846 the Tory Prime Minister, Sir Robert Peel, repealed the Corn Laws, even though this resulted in the splitting of his party and the fall of his government.

Many farmers had predicted disaster if the Corn Laws were repealed, but their worst fears were not immediately realised. There was certainly an increase in the volume of foreign foodstuffs coming into Britain, but the actual total was much less than most people had expected. The Crimean War of 1854–56, the American Civil War of 1861–65 and the Franco-Prussian War of 1870–71 all diminished the world supply of grain and caused shortages, and thus prevented large quantities of cheap corn entering the British market. British farmers therefore continued to enjoy real prosperity, and most of them began to assume that the good times would go on indefinitely.

35 A portable steam-engine and threshing machine. Steam-engines were too heavy to move over the fields—they sunk down—so they were set at the edges of the field to haul machinery back and forth

Farm Workers

Yet if the years after the Agrarian Revolution right down to the 1870s were in the main good ones for the farmers, they were years of distress and hardship for those countryfolk who did not have land of their own and who were forced to work as agricultural labourers. The larger part of this class of labourers had come into existence after the enclosures, for those villagers who had only a few strips in the open fields and who were given only a small piece of land as a consolidated holding were often too poor to pay for the hedges and fences required to enclose their land. Most of them were therefore forced to sell their land and to become agricultural labourers or go into the new factory towns to seek employment.

Those villagers who remained to work as labourers on the farms of their neighbours soon found themselves in a desperate plight. The wages paid were pitifully low, and in the last years of the eighteenth century many men were receiving only 37½p a week. To prevent the labourers from starving, therefore, magistrates began giving them a dole from the poor rate to supplement their wages, the dole rising or falling according to the price of bread.

Although the magistrates had excellent intentions, the paying of a dole to farm labourers had disastrous results. It had the effect of keeping wages down, for farmers knew that no matter how poorly they paid their workers, they would not starve. It also brought about the demoralisation of the workers themselves, for

36 Smithfield Cattle Show in 1845

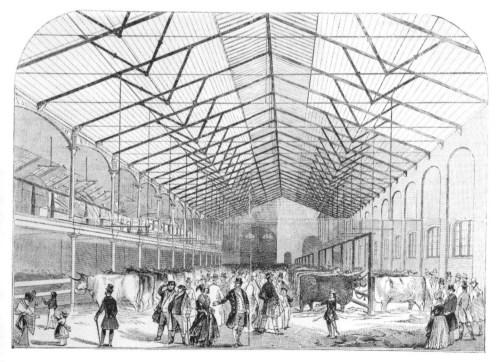

37 Pauper farm workers receiving a dole from a parish officer in the 1830s

men felt that they were living on charity, and they knew that if they tried to better themselves and obtained higher wages, then their dole would be reduced.

The hopelessness of the farm labourers' position at the end of the eighteenth century led many men to seek an escape in drink. Their general feelings of despair were vividly described by a writer of the time when he pictured a labourer sitting in the village ale-house bemoaning his fate. 'If I am diligent, shall I have land for a cow? If I am frugal, shall I have half an acre for potatoes? You offer me no motives; you have nothing but a parish officer and the workhouse. Bring me another pot!'

After the ending of the Napoleonic Wars in 1815, the lives of the farm workers became, if anything, even more miserable. By the end of the 1820s many labourers were so desperate that they joined together in bands to burn hayricks and to smash machinery as a means of registering their protest. Such actions, however, did nothing to win them better conditions, and those who fell into the hands of the authorities were punished severely.

38 Farm labourers destroying machinery

Just how harsh the magistrates of those days could be is shown by the fate of a certain farm worker named George Wren. A hayrick had been burned near Uckfield in 1830, and Wren was arrested. He had helped to put out the blaze, but a footprint of his was found on the other side of the rick from where he had been carrying water. This was the only evidence against him, but nevertheless he was found guilty and sentenced to death, the punishment for arson at this time. The unfortunate Wren was hanged shortly afterwards, but his innocence was proved some years later when the real culprit confessed on his death bed.

While some farm workers were resorting to violence and rick burning, others sought to gain higher wages by forming trade unions. Unions had been made legal in 1825, but their activities were still severely restricted. Thus when workers in the village of Tolpuddle in Dorset formed themselves into the Friendly Society of Agricultural Labourers in 1834, they were prosecuted because they had taken an oath of loyalty to the society, such oaths being illegal. George Loveless, the men's leader, and five of his companions were found guilty and sentenced to seven years' transportation. There was a great public outcry at the harshness of the sentence, and the 'Tolpuddle Martyrs', as they were called, were granted a free pardon in 1836. Yet though the men were freed, this whole affair, together with the terrible penalties inflicted on such men as George Wren, cowed the farm labourers and prevented them from making further attempts to improve their conditions for many years.

In 1834, the same year as the prosecution of the Tolpuddle Martyrs, the government took steps to deal with the growing problem of poverty in the country, but its actions served only to increase the misery of the agricultural workers. It passed a New Poor Law which prohibited the granting of poor relief to supplement wages. Anyone in need was forced to enter a workhouse, and the conditions in the 'Poverty Prisons', as the workhouses were called, were appalling. The discipline was harsh, the diet was poor, and husbands, wives and children were separated from each other and forced to live in different buildings.

The government hoped that the ending of poor relief would force farmers to raise wages, but throughout the 1830s, 40s and 50s wages still remained at a very low level. Yet miserable as were the lives of the ordinary farm workers, they were very much better than those of the gangs of pauper men, women and children who worked on the farms of the Eastern Counties of England. These gangs were recruited by contractors who hired them out to farmers, and they often included young children of six years old. They worked for as long as fourteen hours a day, and sometimes an overseer with a whip followed them about the fields to see that they did not slack. One old lady who had, as a child, been put in one of these gangs at the age of eight recalled later that when she went to work in a factory in Leeds 'it felt like heaven'. Fortunately, however, a Gang Act was passed in 1869 which removed the worst abuses of this practice.

The 1860s at last saw some improvement in the conditions of the ordinary agricultural workers. Wages were beginning to rise, and then in 1871 the

THE

VICTIMS OF WHIGGERY;

BEING

A STATEMENT

OF THE

PERSECUTIONS EXPERIENCED

BY THE

DORCHESTER LABOURERS;

THEIR TRIAL, BANISHMENT, &c. &c.

ALSO

REFLECTIONS

UPON THE

PRESENT SYSTEM OF TRANSPORTATION,

WITH AN

ACCOUNT OF VAN DIEMAN'S LAND,

ITS CUSTOMS, LAWS, CLIMATE, PRODUCE, AND INHABITANTS.

DEDICATED (WITHOUT PERMISSION) TO LORDS MELBOURNE, GREY, RUSSELL, BROUGHAM, AND JUDGE WILLIAMS.

BY GEORGE LOVELESS,

ONE OF THE DORCHESTER LABOURERS.

ANY PROFITS RESULTING FROM THE SALE OF THIS PAMPHLET WILL BE DEVOTED TO THE GENERAL FUND FOR THE RELIEF OF THE FAMILIES OF THE DORCHESTER LABOURERS.

LONDON:

PUBLISHED UNDER THE DIRECTION OF THE CENTRAL DORCHESTER COMMITTEE,
BY EFFINGHAM WILSON, 88, ROYAL EXCHANGE.
H. HETHERINGTON, 126, STRAND;
CLEAVE, 1, SHOE LANE; STRANGE, 21, PATERNOSTER ROW,
AND TO BE HAD OF ALL BOOKSELLERS.

Price Fourpence.

government passed an act fully legalising trade unions. In 1872 a local union was formed in Warwickshire by a worker named Joseph Arch, and by 1874 it had become the National Agricultural Labourers' Union with a membership of 86,000. Almost as soon as it was formed the new Union demanded better wages and conditions, and its campaign met with some success. Within a few years the average weekly wage had risen to 73p, and the standard of living of the agricultural worker rose to a much more respectable level.

The very success of the agricultural workers, however, alarmed the farmers and aroused their hostility. They came to hate the very name of Joseph Arch, and anyone who assisted him was in danger of being persecuted. Thus one smallholder in Oxfordshire who entertained him had his tenancy terminated and was forced to move to a different district because he had 'harboured a dangerous rebel'. A schoolmaster who acted as chairman at one of Arch's meetings found that the local farmers removed their sons from his school.

Such actions did not entirely satisfy the farmers, however, for they were determined to destroy the Union. In 1874, therefore, a number of them joined together and dismissed those of their workers who were members of the Union. After a bitter struggle the labourers were defeated, and many of them left the Union so that they might return to work. The membership of the Union dropped alarmingly, and by 1889 there were only about 4,000 members left. Nevertheless the Union had one further success in 1884 when it played an important part in persuading the government to grant the vote to agricultural workers.

40 This woodcut appeared on handbills circulated among farm labourers in the West of England to convene union meetings during 1874–5

7 Hard Times for Farmers

Although they were unwilling to grant better wages and conditions to their farm workers, the farmers themselves continued to enjoy considerable prosperity throughout the 1850s and 1860s. Many felt that the good times would go on indefinitely and that they could look forward to a bright future of steady growth and advances. But somewhere about 1875 the Golden Age suddenly came to an end, and large numbers of farmers found themselves in serious difficulties. There was a series of bad harvests, and in several districts the grain crops were almost completely ruined. A succession of disasters caught many farmers unprepared, and some were ruined.

Competition from Abroad

British farmers had recovered from bad harvests before this time and would certainly have done so again, but a new and much more dangerous threat to British agriculture appeared in those years. The American Civil War had ended in 1865, and in 1869 the Americancs completed the first railway across the continent. This opened up the vast prairie land of the Middle West, and grain and cereals from the huge farms there could now be transported at low prices to the coast and then across the Atlantic.

In the American Middle West, too, there was some of the most fertile land in the world. On farms equipped with modern machinery and covering vast acres, the American farmers could produce wheat much more cheaply than their counter-parts in Britain and other countries, and after about 1875 this cheap American wheat began to pour into the British market. Its price was much lower than the British grain, and with no import duties to keep it out, it drastically undercut the British product. Prices slumped, and farmers discovered that their profits had completely vanished.

In the face of this competition, many British farmers were forced out of business. Worst affected were the wheat growing areas like Essex and Norfolk, and in such districts there were several bankruptcies. So serious did the situation become that farmers there were forced to cut their production of wheat to a minimum, and between 1872 and 1900 over $2\frac{1}{2}$ million acres of arable land were turned over to grass and pasture.

Early in the 1880s those farmers who had been concentrating on cattle-rearing and beef production and who had consequently been less affected than the wheat producers also began to find their positions threatened. In 1880 the first refrigerated ship carrying meat from Australia arrived at London, and another area of the farming industry was under attack. Australia and New Zealand could produce

meat much more cheaply than British farmers, and now that their products could be transported to the British market in good condition they could again undercut the British producers. Cattle from the great ranches of the American West were also being poured into the British market, and thus the British farmers engaged in the production of beef and mutton were faced with a grim and even desperate situation.

Further threats to British farmers at this time came from agricultural producers in Denmark and other countries on the Continent. The Danes found their own position undermined by the import of cheap grain crops from America, and they turned to dairy farming. So efficient were their farming methods that they produced cheese and butter at extremely low costs. Britain became their main market, and Danish butter and cheese came to undercut the British produce. Once again another area of British farming was being damaged by competition from overseas farmers.

By the early 1890s British farming was in a serious plight. The government appointed a Royal Commission in 1893, and its report told a depressing story of farmers being ruined and of a continuous decline in agricultural production. In 1895 the worst point was reached when the price of wheat fell to £1.15 per imperial quarter, the lowest figure for 150 years.

In the great depression that had struck British agriculture, farmers of all grades and descriptions were affected. Thus some of the wealthiest farmers in the large farms of Norfolk and Essex lost their fortunes and were made bankrupt. The small farmers, too, suffered severely, and many of them were forced to give up their holdings and move to the towns to find work.

Those small farmers who struggled on often lived a life of extreme hardship, and they and their families worked long hours to win a bare living from their fields. The harsh conditions and the difficulties experienced by many small farmers at the end of the century is vividly described in a famous Scottish novel, *Sunset Song*, by Lewis Grassic Gibbon. It portrays a farming community in Kincardine, and there one can see how a series of disasters like the death of a cow or the burning of a byre or stable could drive a small farmer to despair and ruin. Such men were often wonderful characters, and it was a real tragedy that the difficulties in agriculture should be forcing so many of them away from the countryside into the towns and to the countries overseas.

42 A farm in Denmark. Danish farmers were ready to adapt and specialise in dairy products when American competition threatened their grain markets

Many landlords, too, suffered severely from the general depression in agriculture. They often found if difficult to replace those of their tenants who had gone bankrupt, and consequently they were forced to make drastic reductions in the rents they imposed. The incomes from their estates were slashed, and many were therefore forced to sell up. The new owners were often men who had made fortunes in business or industry and who wished to possess land to enhance their social prestige. Sometimes they were prepared to run their estates at a loss so that they could have a country house where they could entertain and impress their friends.

British Farmers Fight Back

Despite all the gloom and depression, however, there were some British farmers who were able to survive and even to prosper. Thus in the dairy farming areas of the West country, of Wales and of Scotland, energetic farmers found ways of overcoming their problems and difficulties. Since most of the dairy farms employed few labourers and were operated by the farmer and his family, they were thus able to cut their expenses. They bought cheap feeding stuffs from abroad, and concentrated on milk production. They could not compete with foreign butter or cheese, but they found in the great industrial centres a ready market for their milk. They also struggled to improve their dairy cattle and to increase the yield, and this allowed many of them to make a reasonable living.

Others farmers managed to survive by switching to market gardening. Again the towns and cities provided excellent markets for fresh vegetables and produce,

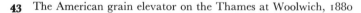

43 The American grain elevator on the Thames at Woolwich, 1880

and considerable profits could be made from this type of farming. Some other farmers concentrated on growing potatoes, and several new and promising varieties were developed. In Ayrshire and other parts of the Lowlands of Scotland a successful and flourishing seed potato industry was developed, and many Scottish farmers made large profits in this trade.

In other districts farmers survived and overcame their difficulties by concentrating on the production of pedigree herds and livestock. Obviously they could not compete with the meat from Australia and other overseas countries, but by producing high quality meat they found a ready market in London and other cities. The Aberdeen-Angus breed continued to flourish in North-East Scotland, while several other breed societies were formed. Thus the Guernsey Cattle Society was founded in 1885, the Welsh Black Cattle Society in 1904, and the British Friesian Cattle Society in 1909. This development allowed British beef producers to meet the challenge from overseas competitors and to retain a substantial share of the market.

Farmers also came to understand the value of co-operation in these difficult times, and in 1908 they formed the National Farmers' Union. Over the years this body has come to include almost 90 per cent of the farmers in the country, and it has provided an invaluable service to its members. It has done much for the individual farmer, for it gives advice to its members on any matter dealing with their farms and farming activities. It also presents the farmers' point of view to the government and seeks to obtain official support and assistance for British farming.

The experiences of all the years of depression and decline, therefore, emphasised the lessons that farmers have learnt throughout the ages: those who were prepared to work hard and adapt their farming practices to changing and difficult conditions could survive and prosper; those who had lost the art of changing and adapting and who wished to go on producing the same wheat crops as formerly, instead of switching over to more profitable lines, went bankrupt.

The failure of some farmers to adapt brought about a considerable movement of personnel throughout the country. Farmers from the West Country or from Ayrshire who had been prospering in dairy farming now moved to the Midlands and Essex where bankruptcies had created a number of vacancies. They obtained their new farms at low rents, and by concentrating on dairy farming and potato production they made a success of their new ventures. They brought with them an independent spirit and a keen appetite for hard work, and these helped them to prosper where their predecessors had failed. This produced a very great change on the farming scene, and in many areas there was almost a complete turn round in the tenants and personnel involved.

Several of the new farmers were extremely shrewd and skilful men, and they were able to build up very large farming enterprises. As the older farmers went bankrupt, they gained possession of their holdings and joined them together to form huge farms. Thus a certain S.W. Farmer of Little Bedwyn in Wiltshire had a holding of some 20,000 acres, while George Baylis of Wyfield Manor had over

12,000 acres in Berkshire and Hampshire. Large estates were also built up in Lincolnshire based on potato growing.

By altering the patterns of their farming, and by dint of hard work and application, therefore, British farmers gradually overcame the worst of their difficulties. In the early years of the twentieth century, moreover, conditions began slowly to improve. There was a recovery in wheat prices, and from 1907 the price never fell below £1.50 per imperial quarter. There was also a boom in industry, and consequently an increasing demand for food from the towns and cities. By this time the weaker farmers had been weeded out, and those who had survived were able to make reasonable profits and to look forward to a continuing prosperity.

And yet the whole period of depression and recovery had produced a tremendous change in the pattern of British agriculture. The total food production of the country had dropped alarmingly, for huge acreages of land had been turned over from arable farming to grasslands, and many herds of beef cattle had been sadly diminished. Thus where Britain's farms had been able to feed the country's population in the early nineteenth century, by 1914 they were producing only enough food for about 40 per cent of the people. This meant that the country was

44 One of the earliest tractors (1902)

becoming more and more dependent on imported foodstuffs. Britain now had to rely on overseas food producers and on her merchant fleet to feed her people.

Farm Workers

The general depression in agriculture had grim consequences for the farm workers of Britain as well as for the farmers and landlords. The small successes their union had gained for them in the 1860s and 1870s soon vanished, and they quickly lost ground. As the farmers' profits dwindled, so the labourers' wages were cut, and once more the farm workers and their families suffered great hardship.

Most farm workers in the last decades of the nineteenth century lived on their employers' farms. The single men and women boarded in the farm house, while married men were given a cottage with some milk, butter and vegetables in addition to their wages. It was customary at this time for farm workers to change their employers every year or even after only six months.

When they wished to move to a new post, the farm workers would normally attend a Hiring Fair. These were held in market towns, and men and women seeking employment stood about in the market place until they were approached and offered work by some farmer. If the labourer accepted, then the farmer gave him a small sum of money, the 'fastening penny', to seal the contract. Sometimes the farm workers would carry an object to indicate their trade, and thus carters might have a whip, milkmaids a pail, thatchers a plait of straw, and shepherds a crook or a piece of wool. In Sussex shepherds were even buried with a lock of sheep's wool so that, we are told, when they reached the Gate of Heaven, St Peter would know why they had not been able to attend church regularly.

As the depression continued and as wages for all types of farm workers were reduced, many men began to seek out some means of supplementing their meagre

45 This heading from a placard of 1874 illustrates the hardships that many farm labourers bore, such as the three months' prison sentence for rabbit poaching, and the fear of spending their old-age in the workhouse. Many farm labourers emigrated during the late nineteenth century

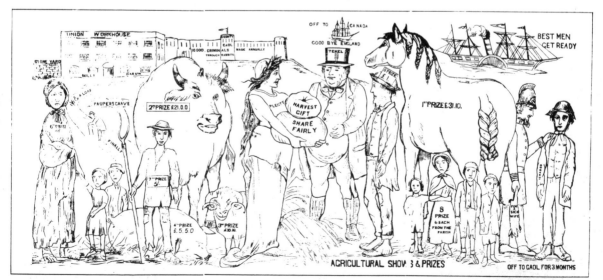

income. Some took over gardens and allotments, and by working long hours in their spare time they were able to maintain their families. Their spirit and sense of humour in the face of adversity is well shown by an old story about one labourer who began to cultivate a deserted kitchen garden and soon had it back in good condition. The local rector noticed the rows of fine vegetables as he passed by one day and observed: 'Ah, Tom, you see what God can do with a garden with a little help'. 'Yes, sir', replied Tom, 'but you should 'a seen it last year when 'E had it to 'Isself'.

Large numbers of farm workers, however, decided to leave the land altogether, and many moved to the towns or emigrated to America or one of the British colonies. The switch over to dairy farming and to sheep farming also brought about a reduction in the demand for farm workers, and many lost their jobs. In all about a third of the labouring population working on the land left farming between 1875 and 1900, and the process that had begun in earlier centuries was intensified. More and more, Britain became a country of towns and cities and factories, with only a tiny fraction of its population living and working on the land.

The departure of such large numbers of people from the countryside completely changed the character of many parts of the country. On an estate near Ramsbury in Wiltshire, for example, some 4,000 acres of arable land were turned into a huge sheep ranch. The hamlet of Snape had been situated on this estate, and in the 1880s it contained a chapel, fourteen cottages and a school attended by 44 children. By 1921, however, the village was deserted, and only a shepherd and his dog remained.

46 A farm labourer's cottage in 1872

8 War and Depression

While British farmers were struggling to overcome all their difficulties in the years after 1875, the country itself was faced with very grave problems. The growth of German power on the Continent came to threaten Britain's position, and by 1900 they were serious rivals. Germany had begun to build a powerful navy, and this threat to Britain's control of the seas alarmed the British people. Britain speeded up her own building of warships, and a great naval arms race was begun.

By the beginning of the twentieth century, too, Europe had been divided into two great competing alliances with Austria and Germany on one side, and France and Russia on the other. In 1904 Britain made an agreement, or Entente, with France, and in the years that followed she grew ever closer to that country. There were several dangerous international crises between 1905 and 1913, and then finally in 1914 the countries of Europe plunged into the First World War. Britain was soon involved when Germany invaded Belgium, and she joined in on the side of France and Russia.

The First World War

With the outbreak of war, it was very quickly seen that the decline in the production of food in Britain which had been going on since about 1880 had placed this country in an extremely vulnerable position. A large percentage of the nation's food now had to be brought by sea from other countries, and these overseas supplies were completely open to attack. Germany had constructed a large fleet of submarines or U-Boats, and these began to launch fierce attacks on Britain's merchant shipping.

Britain had not been really prepared for the German submarine attacks, and as the campaign against our shipping was intensified, it became more and more difficult for the Navy to maintain essential supplies. In 1915 885,000 tons of shipping were lost, and in 1916 a further 1,232,000 tons were sunk. In 1917 the position became even more desperate, and in April of that year 875,000 tons of shipping were lost. Only six weeks' supply of wheat remained in the country, and many officials feared that Britain would be starved into surrender.

Faced by this threat to the country's very existence, the government sought desperately for an answer to the German attacks. At sea it introduced the convoy system in 1917, with large numbers of merchant ships sailing together under naval protection, and this measure cut down the losses dramatically. At home it set about increasing the domestic production of food, and in 1916 it decided to take over control of farming policy. District Committees were set up in all areas to direct the work of the farms and to tell farmers which crops to grow.

The main aim of the government's wartime agricultural policy was to increase the acreage growing wheat and potatoes, for these crops produce much more food from a given area of land than cattle or sheep. Guaranteed prices for wheat and potatoes were laid down, and the farmers were called upon to plough up the lands that had reverted to pasture during the previous forty years. This was no easy task, for many farm workers had already joined the services, but the government helped solve this problem by forming a Women's Land Army. With the assistance of this force and of large numbers of schoolboys and other volunteers, the farmers were able to meet the targets set for them. By 1918 the production of wheat was 54 per cent higher than in 1916, barley 17 per cent, oats 38 per cent and potatoes 68 per cent higher. Thus the efforts of the farmers of Britain played a most important part in saving the country from defeat.

Not surprisingly the increased acreage and the increased production of foodstuffs brought prosperity to the farmers, for they had no difficulty in selling every last peck of their crops. However, it would be wrong to think that the country's misfortunes brought them great wealth. The government was well aware that prices would soar in times of such scarcity, and therefore it fixed maximum prices for bread and other foodstuffs in an attempt to prevent the cost of living from rising too sharply. Thus, though the farmers' position was immeasurably better than it had been in the pre-war years, they did not make the large profits that some persons engaged in the armaments industry, for example, were able to secure.

47 A wartime convoy of merchant ships in the Atlantic

Some farmers, too, were rather unhappy about all the regulations turned out by the District Committees, for they felt that they knew better than any officials what their lands could best produce. Thus various tales began to circulate about the alleged foolishness of the Committees' orders. One story relates how a particular farmer received a letter telling him to begin planting his potato crop. He replied that he was unable to do so since he was in the middle of the lambing season. The Committee then sent another letter repeating their instruction, and again the farmer replied that he could not comply. Soon afterwards a telegram was delivered to him which read: 'Cease lambing. Begin planting immediately'. Most of the stories, however, were wildly exaggerated, for the majority of the members of the District Committees were experienced farmers.

Between the Wars

Despite all the services made by the farmers to the nation in its time of peril, the return of peace in 1918 saw the people of Britain forget all the lessons that the war should have taught them. It had seemed only too evident that it was dangerous for Britain to neglect her own farming and to depend too much on overseas food supplies, but almost everyone save the farmers chose to forget this uncomfortable fact. The prices of wheat and certain other foodstuffs had been guaranteed for a number of years, but when the guarantees expired in 1921, they were not renewed and a policy of Free Trade was once more adopted.

The results were again disastrous for the farmers and the sorry story of the years between 1875 and 1914 were repeated during the 1920s. Once more farmers were forced to reduce their wheat acreage and to turn to dairy farming, market gardening and the raising of pedigree herds. Again there were considerable numbers of farmers going bankrupt, and once more the drift of farmers and farm workers from the land to the towns got under way.

Nevertheless, amidst all the gloom and depression, some men were able to survive and even to prosper. One of these was the famous Wiltshire farmer, Arthur Hosier, who had switched over to dairy farming almost as soon as the war finished. His herds brought him in substantial profits, but he was not satisfied, for he was a restless man, ever on the look-out for new ways of improving his farming. Early in the 1920s he invented a movable milking shed which could be taken to the fields where the cows were grazing. This saved a great deal of time and labour, for no longer had the cows to be led backwards and forwards from distant fields to the milking sheds. Since Hosier also kept his cattle in the fields night and day, summer and winter, the cows manured the land where they were grazing and he was saved the labour and expense of carting dung from the cow-sheds to the fields. His new methods soon proved a great success, and in a few years they were being copied by farmers all over the country.

Though men of Arthur Hosier's ability and ingenuity were rare, most farmers showed the same determination to overcome their difficulties. Patiently they waited for the return of better times, and their patience was soon rewarded, for the policy of Free Trade which had been largely responsible for the decline of British agriculture since 1875 was not to survive for very much longer. In 1931 Britain, together with the rest of the world, experienced a severe depression, and international trade came almost to a standstill. Britain found that other countries had practically stopped buying her exports, even though she was still importing a large volume of goods. She was therefore forced to abandon Free Trade and to introduce measures to protect her industries.

In the light of this new situation, it soon became clear that the country could no longer afford to go on allowing foreign foodstuffs free access to the British market. Import duties were placed on many foods from foreign countries, although supplies from the British Empire were usually exempted from these duties. Quotas were also imposed on the imports of bacon, beef, pork, mutton and tinned and processed milk from foreign countries. These measures permitted a modest expansion in the imports of food from the Empire, but the total volume of imports from abroad was reduced. Thus British farmers, especially those concerned in the production of those foodstuffs on which quotas had been placed, had rather better prospects of making a success of their enterprises.

Further assistance for farmers was provided by the introduction of subsidies for producers of sugar-beet, wheat, oats, barley and fat cattle. Support for sugar-beet had been introduced in 1925, while subsidies for wheat growers were provided for by the Wheat Act of 1932. This assistance was extended to the producers of oats and barley by the Agriculture Act of 1937. A temporary subsidy for fat cattle was provided in 1934, and this was made permanent by the Livestock Industry Act of 1937. Important as these various subsidies were, however, the grants awarded were not very large, and in the three years 1935–38 the total yearly subsidies averaged only about £13 million.

48 A portable milking unit

Another measure taken by the government to assist our farmers was the setting up of Marketing Boards under the terms of the Agricultural Act of 1931. If the majority of the farmers producing a particular commodity so desired, then a selling organisation or Marketing Board could be established. Once a Marketing Board had been established for a commodity, moreover, all farmers producing it were required to sell their goods through the Board. In the years that followed, Marketing Boards for milk, potatoes, hops, pigs, wool and eggs were established. Such Boards did much to improve the farmer's position, for often in the past the individual farmer had been at the mercy of traders and merchants and was forced to accept any low price he might be offered. Now, however, all farmers were

49 Research workers at an agricultural college

combined into one organisation, and they were therefore in a much stronger position to bargain and to obtain better prices.

The government also showed its increased interest in farming at this time by setting up an Agricultural Research Council in 1931 to supervise the work of the many research institutes that had been founded in earlier years. Many farmers, however, were not very impressed by this step, for they felt that the scientists working in research institutes knew nothing about the real problems of farming and that their discoveries and inventions were of little practical value. One small farmer, for example, described a visit to a research institute where he found two experts engaged in inventing a meter to measure the draught in milking sheds! Nevertheless, though much of the work of the research institutes has seemed pointless to ordinary farmers, yet they have made many important discoveries and have done invaluable work in applying scientific principles to farming.

Aided by such measures, British agriculture slowly recovered from the worst of the depression. Even by 1939, however, it was still far from prosperous, and many farmers still found it difficult to make a reasonable living from their farms. Agricultural production increased by only about one sixth during the 1930s, while between 1929 and 1939 almost 145,000 of the workers employed in agriculture, or about 20 per cent of the total, left the land. Clearly the position of British farming was still far from being a satisfactory one.

The Second World War
Once again, however, the situation was transformed when Britain was involved in another great conflict, the Second World War (1939–45). During the 1930s Germany, under Hitler, had embarked on a policy of expansion in Europe, and one after the other the Rhineland, Austria and Czechoslovakia were seized. For a time Britain and France tried to come to terms with Hitler, but when Germany attacked Poland in 1939 the two countries declared war.

Germany had again concentrated on building a large fleet of submarines, and now they took up stations in the Atlantic to attack supplies sailing for Britain. But the government had learnt its lesson from the experiences of the First World War, and without delay it took over control of agriculture and took steps to increase the home-produced food supplies. Agricultural Executive Committees were set up in all areas, and a crash programme of ploughing up grassland was inaugurated. The target set for the first year of the war was the seemingly impossible one of 2 million extra acres, but by ploughing night and day the farmers achieved their objective. The authorities were far from satisfied, however, and before the end of the war in 1945 a total of $6\frac{1}{2}$ million extra acres were ploughed up and sown with crops of wheat, barley, oats and potatoes to feed Britain's wartime population.

As in the First World War, the farms of Britain experienced an acute shortage of labour between 1939 and 1945 when many skilled workers left to serve with the armed forces, but the government did much to overcome this by drafting prisoners of war to the fields, by recruiting volunteer and schoolboy labour, and by raising a Women's Land Army of some 90,000 members. A few farmers were critical of the volunteers and the Land Girls, but most found that they performed their new tasks amazingly well. The Land Girls in particular, it seems, surprised everyone by their ability to undertake every kind of farm work, no matter how heavy or dirty. Some even worked as rat catchers, and one girl, an ex-dress designer, is said to have caught 327 rats in a Yorkshire granary. This achievement was clearly a most valuable contribution to the war effort, for 300 rats can eat 3 tons of wheat a year!

An amusing story was told by an East Anglian farmer about one of these rat catchers of the Women's Land Army which illustrates perfectly how at first farmers were rather apprehensive about the Land Girls and how later they came to respect their work. 'A girl came into my yard one morning', he explained, 'and said to me, "You've got rats here, haven't you, mister?" and I said, "Well, maybe half a dozen, but they won't hurt you, missy", and she said, "It's not me I'm worrying about". She took a look at the barn and the drains and said, "You've got more than half a dozen, mister, but leave 'em to me, I'll fix 'em". Then she opened a sack and started bringing out bait and poison. I said, "What d'you think you're up to?" and she replied, "Don't you worry, mister, I'm the rat catcher. The Committee (Agricultural Executive Committee) sent me down". But I did worry. I flew round to my man and I said, "Lock up all the stock, Alf, there's a female rat-catcher here and she'll slaughter the lot!" He was as frightened as I was, but we needn't have bothered, the girl knew her job all right. Later that week she came to me and said, "Take a look at the barn, mister". I did and there were 60

50 Ploughing up school play fields during the Second World War

dead rats laid out in the prettiest pattern you ever saw. And I never knew we'd got that many in the whole village'.

In addition to recruiting new kinds of farm workers, the government also encouraged farmers to make a greater use of machines in order to overcome the shortage of labour. In the early months of the war, of course, many farmers were without machines and modern equipment, and thus they had to display considerable ingenuity in carrying out the government's programme. One Cotswold sheep farmer, for example, won a tremendous local reputation for himself by inventing a new 'machine' when he was ordered to plant 10 acres of potatoes.

51 Recruiting poster for the Women's Land Army

NATIONAL SERVICE   w/33

10,000 Women Wanted For Farm Work

A FREE OUTFIT, high boots, breeches, overall and hat.

MAINTENANCE during training.

TRAVELLING expenses in connection with the work.

WAGES 18/- per week, or the district rate, whichever is the higher.

MAINTENANCE during terms of unemployment up to four weeks.

HOUSING personally inspected and approved by the Women's War Agricultural Committee in each County.

WORK on carefully selected farms.

PROMOTION, good work rewarded by promotion and higher pay.

AFTER THE WAR, special facilities for settlement at home or overseas.

DON'T DELAY ENROL TO-DAY

Application Forms may be had at all Post Offices & Employment Exchanges.

DIRECTOR GENERAL OF NATIONAL SERVICE,
ST. ERMINS, S.W. 1.

One of his neighbours happened to be passing his farm one day when he heard 'a noise like a gurt clock'. 'I didn't know where it came from', he related later, 'till I looked over the wall. Then I seen old Jesse. He'd got a three-furrow plough he was ridin' on and a tin bath full of spuds in his arms. He'd raked up an old chimney-pot from somewhere and got it wedged between his knees. There was some sort of gadget stuck on the wheel somewhere which rang a bell every time it turned round, and each time this bell rang old Jesse dropped a tarter down the chimney. "Jesse", I said, "that's as neat a contraption as I've seen anywhere".'

Soon, however, the need for such gadgets and contraptions declined as under the government's directives our factories began to turn out large numbers of tractors and farming machines. Many more were imported from the United States, and by 1944 there were as many as 175,000 tractors on the farms of Britain, while there were at least 2,000 combine harvesters. Britain had become the most highly mechanised farming country in the world, and with the new machines our farmers and volunteer workers were able to produce the huge wartime harvests which did so much to bring us victory in 1945. Once again it had been shown just how vital our farming was to the security of the nation, but as the end of the war drew near, many farmers began to fear that the government's assistance would not be continued in peacetime and that farming would once more experience a post-war depression.

52 An improvised motor-driven plough in the early years of the Second World War

9 A New Deal for Farmers

Despite the fears and misgivings of many farmers when the Second World War ended in 1945, most of the people of Britain and most of the politicians of all parties were determined that agriculture should not be allowed to decline as it had done after the First World War. Almost everyone was at last convinced that a thriving farming industry was essential to the country's welfare. We could not afford to be dependent on imports in the future lest once more we faced starvation when our supplies from abroad were threatened. It was also realised that the rapid increase in the world's population must create a bigger demand for food, and that food supplies from abroad might eventually become more difficult to obtain.

New Agricultural Policies

The task of working out a new policy for British farming fell to the Labour Government appointed in 1945, for the Labour Party won the General Election held at the end of the war. The government did not wish to halt the imports of cheap food from abroad, however, for the industrial population of Britain had grown accustomed to cheap butter, meat, mutton, and dairy produce from the Commonwealth and from countries all over the world. It therefore had to discover a new method of assisting farmers, and at length it brought forward such a method in the Agriculture Act of 1947, one of the great landmarks in the post-war history of British farming.

By the 1947 Act the government introduced the principles of guaranteed prices and guaranteed markets for the most important farm products including fat stock, milk, eggs, wheat, barley, oats, rye, potatoes and sugar-beet, with wool being added a few years later. Each year an annual review was to be held to fix minimum prices for the various commodities during the following seasons. Thus farmers knew before they began production in any one year that they would be able to sell all their crops and livestock, and that they would at least be able to secure the agreed minimum prices for them.

The authorities, however, did not wish to provide support for incompetent farmers, and therefore in the annual reviews their general efficiency was to be taken into account. All the costs of producing the particular commodities were examined carefully, and then the minimum prices were fixed to ensure that only those farmers who kept improving their productivity would really benefit. Agricultural Executive Committees were also established in each county to supervise the efficiency of British farms and farming. These Committees could exercise an oversight of the farms in their district, and if the land was not being cared for properly they could dispossess the farmer concerned.

Such measures were to be exceptional, however, and indeed the Labour Government took steps to give the farmers greater security of tenure than they had formerly enjoyed. In earlier centuries farmers could be evicted by their landlord when their leases expired, and often they received no compensation for any improvements they might have made. A particularly shocking example of an excellent farmer losing the tenancy of his farm occurred in Scotland in the late nineteenth century. A certain family named Hope had farmed in East Lothian for three generations with such success that their reputation was known throughout Britain and other countries. But when one of the family, George Hope, stood as a Liberal candidate for Parliament, his landlord, a Conservative, punished him by refusing to renew his lease. Not all landlords, however, were so mean spirited, and some would not press their tenants for payment of their rent in difficult years. One Aberdeenshire landlord, for example, when told by one of his tenants that his rent was too high, replied 'How can that be, John? You've paid no rent at all for a long time past'.

Nevertheless, though many landlords were generous and considerate, farmers disliked a system whereby they could lose the tenancy of their farms whenever their lease expired. They pressed for a change in the law, and in 1920 their position was improved when an Act was passed stating that a tenant must receive compensation, amounting in most cases to one year's rent, if the landlord refused

53 A modern sheep farmer on Salisbury Plain. By using a tractor he can take responsibility for several flocks over a large area

to renew his lease. In 1948 the farmer's position was further strengthened by an Act which in effect gave him security of tenure for his lifetime so long as he worked his land efficiently. A landlord could end a farmer's tenancy only if he could prove that the land was deteriorating under his management, or if the landlord himself required the land for certain specified purposes.

Several further Acts were also passed to complete the Labour Government's agricultural policy. In 1946, for instance, a Hill Farming Act was introduced, and by this and other measures subsidies were given for cattle and sheep in hill farms. Grants were also available for drainage, for applying lime to fields, and for restoring lands that had been flooded. Then in 1949 an Agricultural Marketing Act was introduced to reorganise the Marketing Boards for milk, eggs and other foodstuffs. More government nominees were appointed to the Boards and the Government Minister for food had stronger powers over the operations of the Marketing Boards.

54 Spraying a wheat field

The government's new support policy for British farming as embodied in the 1947 Agriculture Act and the various other measures was extremely ingenious. It meant that cheap food imports from Australia, New Zealand, the United States and other countries could still be brought into Britain to help keep down the price of food in the shops. But this free entry policy did not ruin the British farmers because they were given various subsidies as well as guaranteed prices and a guaranteed market. If there was a surplus of food on the world markets, then our imports would be cheaper, but the government would have to pay more to the farmers to bring their prices up to the agreed minimum. If world prices were dearer, then the British farmers would get a higher price on the market, but the government would have to pay less to them in support.

The agricultural policies laid down by the Labour Government in the late 1940s have been followed in the main by all the post-war governments, both

55 A modern 'milking parlour'

Labour and Conservative. They have been reasonably successful, and the position of British farmers has been much better than it had been between the Wars or before the First World War. With guaranteed prices and markets in the major foodstuffs, farmers have been able to increase their production and to improve their livestock and the fertility of their lands. The production of foodstuffs has been increased dramatically: in 1972 60 per cent of the food consumed in Britain was produced by British farmers, compared with only 30 per cent in 1938.

Not everyone, however, has supported the post-war agricultural policies. Some critics claim that the annual review and the subsidies to farming place a very great strain on the taxpayer who has to provide the necessary funds. In the late 1940s one Government Minister even declared that the farmers were being 'feather bedded', so large were the grants and subsidies being given to them. But this is definitely a minority view, and most people would admit that British farmers have served the country well in the post-war years, and that the assistance given to them has saved the country a large volume of imports and has thus helped the balance of payments.

The farmers themselves have certainly prospered, but they have not always reaped all the benefits of the increased production on the farms. The government has kept a tight control in the annual reviews, and it has continually kept any increase in minimum prices in check. Thus if there is a substantial rise in the production of any particular commodity, then the subsidies and the minimum prices might be reduced so that the farmer's income does not rise proportionately to his extra efforts and productivity. Indeed many farmers complain that over the years it has become more and more difficult for them to make a reasonable profit from their farms. They have increased their productivity more than most other groups in the community, but their incomes often compare unfavourably with those of people in industry.

Increasing mechanisation has also helped to make the farms of Britain more efficient since 1945, while the more extensive use of new chemical fertilisers and weed controllers had helped to boost production. There has also been a tendency for farms to grow larger, and thus the new farming machinery can be operated more efficiently. In 1966 the government introduced a scheme whereby small farms were to be amalgamated into larger units. Farmers were to be given a golden handshake or lump sum of money if they were prepared to retire at an early age and allow their land to be joined up with other farms.

All this has continued the trend in Britain of people moving away from the land and into the towns. Today, less than 3 per cent of the population are engaged in agriculture, and the drift away from the farms continues. The fact that the diminished farming community of the present time is able to produce a much greater volume of food than the larger farm population before 1939 is a very considerable testimony to the farmers of the country and to the government policies followed since the Second World War.

The Common Market

Nevertheless, although the system of supporting our farmers which we have followed since 1945 has certainly served Britain well, it will have to be drastically altered when Britain enters the European Economic Community. The six countries of France, Germany, Italy, Belgium, Holland and Luxembourg formed the community in 1957, and they have developed a very different agricultural policy from that followed in Britain. Thus instead of permitting the import of cheap foodstuffs from outside the Community, the Common Market countries have placed duties on imports. For many commodities there are guaranteed prices, and these are fixed at a high level to ensure the farmers a fair return for their produce. All the countries impose common tariffs on food imports, and these go into a fund which is used to provide grants and support for the farmers of the Community.

Britain's first application to join the European Economic Community was submitted in 1961, but this was vetoed by France. A second application in 1965 was also vetoed, but a third application in 1970 resulted in successful negotiations. In October 1971 the British Parliament agreed in principle to enter into the Community, and the way was prepared for legislation to make the required changes adapting British institutions to those of the Community.

56 An advanced 'super' combine harvester. Modern farmers must know how to operate and maintain such equipment in addition to the more traditional farming skills

During the negotiations Britain agreed to accept the agricultural policies of the Community, and this will inevitably produce profound changes in British farming. No longer will cheap food imports from the Commonwealth and elsewhere be allowed into the British market, and thus the prices of food in the shops will rise substantially. The levies placed on the imports of foodstuffs will go into the Community's funds, and since Britain is still a very large importer of foodstuffs we will be paying out considerable sums of money to support agriculture on the Continent.

For British farmers, however, entry into the Common Market could probably bring a further period of progress and prosperity. They will certainly face strong

57 Work on a French farm. Many French farms remain small and unmodernised. This is reflected in the agricultural policies of the Common Market

competition from Continental farmers, but with guaranteed prices for their products and with protection against competition from countries outside the Community many farmers in Britain could do very well indeed. There will be great opportunities for them in the home and Continental markets, and it is most probable that agricultural production will be considerably increased.

Farm Workers

In the same way that British farmers have enjoyed greater prosperity since 1945, so, too, the conditions of farm workers and labourers have steadily improved. Since the beginning of the century, indeed, the wages of farm labourers have tended to rise and fall as farming has been more or less prosperous. Thus while wages remained low up until 1914, they rose substantially during the First World War. There was some small improvement between 1919 and 1939, but then during the Second World War wages rose to new heights. Since 1945 the earnings of farm workers have risen steadily until by 1972 the national minimum wage had reached a level of £16.20 per week.

This improvement in the wages of farm workers was brought about not only by the increasing prosperity of British farming, but also by the action of the government in setting up Agricultural Wages Boards and by the farm workers themselves through their unions. Wages Boards for fixing a minimum wage in each county were established during the First World War, and although they were abolished at the end of the war, they were revived in 1924. During the Second World War two National Wages Boards were established, one for England and Wales, and the other for Scotland, and by the Agricultural Wages (Regulation) Act of 1947 these Boards were made permanent. The Boards establish national minimum wages and hours of work which will apply to farm workers throughout the respective countries.

The Farm Workers' Unions, too, have helped to obtain better conditions for their members. The earlier Unions had often been weak and ineffective, but during the First World War several of the older unions amalgamated to form the National Union of Agricultural Workers. This new Union has proved most active in advancing the interests of farm workers, and by 1972 it had a membership of 90,000.

Nevertheless, despite all the improvements in the wages and conditions of farm workers, their earnings are still much lower than those received by many workers in industry. One cannot but wonder, therefore, if the community really values the farm worker at his proper worth and gives him a fair return for the contribution he makes to the nation's welfare. Today it is not enough that he should be an expert in all the traditional farming skills, but he must in addition be a skilled mechanic to operate and maintain all the machinery on a modern farm. He must also know something about electricity, have a knowledge of fertilisers, chemicals and drugs, and be familiar with modern scientific methods of breeding and rearing animals.

FARM WORKER WANT £18.
DORSET SAYS £18
DORSET SAYS £18
NION POLICY
£18
40 HOUR
5 DAY WEEK
RATE £13-3-0
43 HOURS

10 Today and Tomorrow

With all the developments in farming that we have traced through the ages, we can see that our system of farming today is changed almost out of all recognition from the way in which our distant ancestors won their living from the soil. It is now highly mechanised, and electricity is being used for more and more purposes. Agriculture is also increasingly a science-based industry. Chemicals are used to promote the growth of plants, to fertilize the soil, and to kill weeds and the bacteria and fungi which attack crops. Animals are given drugs to immunise them against illness, while chickens can be given an injection to make them grow quicker. Now artificial insemination is being practised by more and more farmers, for this enables first-class bulls to father some thousands of calves, the quality of our herds being thereby improved.

In recent years, too, there has been a rapid development of what are known as 'factory farms'. In such farms large numbers of chickens, calves or pigs are kept penned in small cages or small enclosed spaces. There they are given special foodstuffs and drugs to promote rapid growth, and after a relatively short time they are killed for the market. This type of farming has aroused a great deal of criticism, for many people believe it is cruel and that animals should be allowed to roam freely around in the fields and the countryside.

The Way Ahead

In the near future, one can reasonably expect to see further developments and changes in British farming. The tendency is for farms and fields to get bigger so that modern machinery can be used more profitably, and there is every likelihood that this process will continue. Perhaps, too, the farmers in various districts will learn to co-operate more effectively with their neighbours so that they can all obtain the benefits of large-scale production. In the Soviet Union such co-operation is secured through the collective farms which are owned by the State or a group of farmers. It seems that under this system, however, there is less incentive for the individual farmer to work hard, and the British farmer is unlikely to give up willingly the possession or control of his own piece of land.

Whatever changes in farm organisation are eventually introduced into Britain, there seems little doubt that the farmers will be asked to produce a much greater volume of foodstuffs than ever before. The world's population is growing at a spectacular rate, and experts declare that it will reach 6,000 million by the end of this century. Thus there will be an increasing demand for food, and we cannot doubt from their past record that the farmers of Britain will rise to meet the challenge.

83

58 (*opposite*) Farm workers demonstrating to obtain higher wages

Part of the increased future production will undoubtedly come from further improvements and developments in farming techniques. Scientists will continue their efforts to improve seeds and livestock, and one can imagine, too, that many new machines will be invented. Perhaps in the very near future some genius will invent a completely successful potato harvester which will do the work now carried out by large squads of potato lifters!

Further ahead there are all sorts of exciting possibilities. Hitherto we have obtained our food through the medium of plants or animals, but some scientists believe that we could easily produce all the proteins, fats and sugar we require by other means. During the Second World War, for example, German scientists

59 Chicks being fed in a 'factory farm'

discovered a method of synthesising fat from coke! The fat was not very appetising and was very expensive to produce, but nevertheless it was quite edible. Again, some scientists have recently been carrying out experiments to produce fat and protein from tiny plants and yeast cultivated in large tanks placed in the bright sunshine of certain desert areas. These experiments have met with some success, though the costs of production have been very high, and it seems probable, therefore, that one day we shall be able to obtain substantial quantities of food by such methods.

With all the exciting new developments lying ahead on the farming scene, it seems that the outlook for our farmers is reasonably bright, and that farming has

60 Artificial insemination

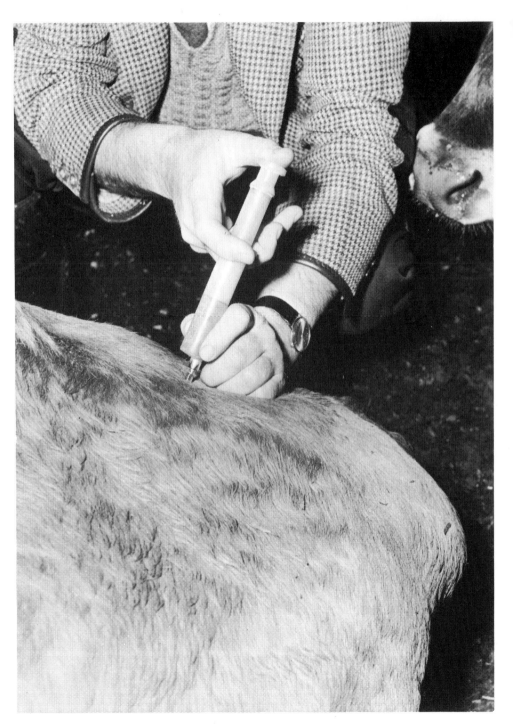

61 A cow receiving an injection to immunise it against disease

much to offer as a career for young people. For farm workers, too, the prospects will be better than they have too often been in the past. As they become ever more skilled in a wide range of activities, and as the demand for their services intensifies, the farm workers should find their wages coming more into line with those of industrial workers. There is a shortage of labour in many areas, and it is unlikely that farm workers will be in any danger of experiencing long periods of un-employment.

Farming in Other Countries

Our study of the history of agriculture has in the main concentrated on British farming, but in other countries the experiences and fortunes of the farmers have often been quite different from those of our own. The crops which a country grows and the type of agriculture it practises depend primarily on its climate and soil. Thus, for example, the wet monsoon lands of China and south-east Asia are particularly suitable for the growing of rice, and the whole system of farming in these regions throughout the centuries has centred on this crop. It is grown in muddy and flooded fields, and it is the main diet of the people in many parts of Asia.

Another important food crop which requires special climatic conditions is sugar. The sugar cane originated in Asia, and from there it spread to Egypt and the Middle East. The Arabs later carried it to North Africa and Spain, and in the fifteenth century the early Spanish explorers took it to the West Indies. There the hot and moist climate provided ideal conditions, and the West Indies have become one of the main sugar-producing regions of the world. In the Middle Ages the people of Britain had used honey as a sweetener, but when we obtained possession of certain West Indian Islands, sugar was increasingly used. Today the bulk of our supplies comes from the West Indies, and during the negotiations for our entry into the Common Market, care was taken to safeguard the interests of the producers there.

In the countries of Europe, too, the pattern of agriculture has been rather different from that in Britain. By and large the same crops have been grown because climatic conditions have been similar, but the pattern of organisation and ownership has been different. Thus in many of the countries of Western Europe there have been more smaller farms than in Britain, and the movement of people from the farms to the towns has been slower. 14 per cent of the work force in the countries of the Common Market are employed in agriculture, as compared with a figure of only 3 per cent in Britain; nearly 50 per cent of the farms of Britain are of over 50 acres in size compared with only about 15 per cent on the Continent. It is this different pattern, of course, which has produced a different system for supporting agriculture in the European Economic Community and has secured greater protection for the Continental farmers through higher tariffs on imports of food.

As has happened in Britain in modern times, so on the Continent and in other countries, too, farming has become more and more mechanised and scientific in recent years. The United States, Canada and Australia have played a leading part in the invention and introduction of farming machines, but even in the under-developed parts of the world changes are taking place. Rice cultivation, for example, is being steadily improved by the introduction of machines, by the breeding of better varieties of plants, and by the discovery of new methods of fertilising the paddy fields. Modern methods are also being applied to the growing and harvesting of the sugar cane.

Playing an important part in improving agriculture in the underdeveloped areas of the world is the Food and Agriculture Organisation (FAO), a special agency of the United Nations. The FAO was established in 1945 to give assistance to the farmers of the world, and since that time it has done an immense amount of good. It has carried out research to improve crops and animals, it has designed better tools for farmers in poorer countries, and it has sought to protect farmers in tropical countries from such diseases as malaria and hookworm.

More a Way of Life
Hitherto we have been concerned principally with farming as a means of providing food for mankind, but we should be underestimating the importance of agriculture in human history if we believed that that was all it involved. We saw earlier how farming activities had helped to develop mathematics, astronomy and the alphabet in Ancient Egypt, and throughout the ages it has been closely linked with almost every aspect of human life and affairs. In medieval times, for instance, the whole way of life of a village centred round the work in the open fields, and the people's games, festivals, songs, dances and customs were all connected with farming.

At other times and in other lands, too, the system of agriculture that was followed helped to influence the lives of the people, and where there was a distinctive type of farming, then this helped to create a particular way of life. Thus the rice-growing areas of China and south-east Asia with their paddy fields and numerous villages witnessed the appearance of a form of civilisation which was very different from that with which we are familiar in Europe. Again, the great cattle ranches of the nineteenth century American West provided the setting for the life and culture of the cowboy with its songs, legends and distinct attitudes to life.

In modern times, of course, the great majority of people in Britain live in towns and work in offices or factories, and thus they are much less influenced by our farming system than our ancestors were. Yet it is a surprising fact that much of our lives are still affected by agriculture and that many of our festivals and holidays are associated with farming. Easter, for instance, was in origin a pagan festival celebrating the coming of spring and the beginning of the spring ploughing.

62 View from a sugar mill on the West Indian Island of St. Kitts showing plantations of sugar-cane. Most of our sugar comes from the West Indies or Australia, but a small proportion is grown in Britain from sugar beet, a root crop, grown mostly in East Anglia and subsidised by the government

Again, our long school holidays in summer were originally given so that boys could return home to help with the harvest.

Many of our traditional songs, too, have a close association with farming. Men and women often sang as they worked in the fields, and the rhythm of their music sprang from the rhythm of the work they were doing. One old Gaelic song, 'The mi sgith', for instance, describes the feelings of the farmer as he cuts bracken. This song is still sung today, and it recaptures for us with its rhythm the movements of the farmers of old as they performed this task in the fields. Many of these old tunes were later used to accompany new folk songs unconnected with farming, but nevertheless they have thereby become part of our national heritage of music.

63 Dutch polder farms on land reclaimed from the sea. It is easy to use modern farm machinery on these flat, large fields

Not only did farm work provide our ancestors with the rhythm of their music, however, but it seems that there was also something about farming and certain aspects of country life which could inspire men to write songs and poetry. Robert Burns, for instance, could declare that 'Corn rigs are bonnie, oh', while his admiration was won by the girl who was 'Coming through the rye'. Modern industry, by contrast, has not often provided such inspiration, and we may wait in vain for some present-day genius to tell us that 'An internal combustion engine is bonnie, oh', or that he has fallen in love with the girl who was 'Walking between the rows of factory machines'.

64 Children following an old custom parade through the village with a plough to collect money on Plough Monday

It can be seen, therefore, that agriculture has meant much more to mankind than the mere producing of food. It has influenced men's thinking and customs, it has helped to develop a distinctive way of life in different ages and in different parts of the world, and it has inspired writers to create wonderful songs and music. The men and women on our farms today can indeed be proud of the work they are doing; for not only are they ensuring that the population of Britain and the world will have enough to eat, but they are also the heirs of a long tradition which is in a sense the tradition of mankind itself.

The Lessons of the Past

Fortunately as heirs of that tradition, we in modern times have the example of the wonderful achievements of our forefathers to help us meet the challenges that face all those engaged in agriculture today. Their triumphs and failures have much to teach us, and we would do well to learn the lessons of the past. One of the most important of these lessons is that almost all the great advances in farming have been brought about by men who were not satisfied with things as they were and who were prepared to carry out experiments to secure improvements. The tribesmen who first thought of taming animals or of planting seed, and the individuals who invented the hoe, the plough, the drilling machine and the combine harvester were all men of genius who were determined to discover a better way of doing things.

One should not, however, underestimate the difficulties which such men had to face when introducing their discoveries. Many people and many farmers are conservative by nature and are content to leave things as they are. If their crops have been grown in a certain rotation in the past, then they insist that this is the way they should always be grown and that there is no need for change. Every new invention or alteration in farming methods is met with opposition and often with a great deal of hostility. Thus, for example, Jethro Tull found that his workers would not use his new seed drill, and indeed some of them even attempted to destroy the machine.

The introduction of potatoes into this country was another development that was at first greeted with great suspicion, and many farmers refused to grow them. The story is told that Macdonald of Clanranald in 1743 ordered his clansmen in South Uist to plant the new crop. At first they refused, and it was only when some of them were imprisoned that they agreed to do so. But when the first crops were harvested, they brought all the potatoes to the chief's house declaring that though he might force them to grow them, he could not force them to eat them! In the same way there was at first great hostility to the drinking of tea, and some writers denounced tea as a 'demoralising drug' and described tea-drinking as a 'pernicious habit'.

Yet before we laugh too much at our ancestors for these foolish attitudes, we should ask ourselves if we are really very much better today. We live in an age when we are accustomed to new inventions as our forefathers never were, but many of us are still suspicious of change and new ideas. There is, for example, a considerable opposition to the use of chemical fertilisers. Many people claim that such fertilisers are 'unnatural' and that they must be harmful to us. They seem, however, to ignore the fact that there are simply not nearly enough 'natural' fertilisers available to grow the crops that we require to feed the world's population today.

The lesson, therefore, is clear. Modern farmers must not resemble those of our ancestors who were described by one writer as a 'race of rural robots'. Instead they must be ready to accept new ideas and to make use of all the latest findings of agricultural science to increase their production and the yield of their fields. In this way they will be performing an invaluable service to the community, for as Jonathan Swift said in *Gulliver's Travels*, he who makes 'two ears of corn, or two blades of grass, to grow on a spot where only one, grew before deserves better of mankind and does more essential service to his country than the whole race of politicians put together'.

65 An improved type of barley produced by crop mutation at the International Atomic Energy Agency near Vienna

FURTHER READING

Burbridge, E. W.	*The Story of Agriculture* (Pitman).
Butcher, T. K.	*Country Life* (Batsford).
Crowther, J. G.	*The Story of Agriculture* (Hamish Hamilton).
Donaldson, J. G. S. & F.	*Farming in Britain Today* (Allen Lane, The Penguin Press).
Ernle, Lord	*English Farming Past and Present* (Heinemann).
Franklin, T. Bedford	*A History of Agriculture* (Bell).
Franklin, T. Bedford	*A History of Scottish Farming* (Nelson).
Hall, C. J.	*A Short History of English Agriculture and Rural Life* (Black).
Ed. Howells, R.	*The Farming Series* (Rendel).
Kitchen, F.	*Brother to an Ox* (Dent).
Lee, Norman E.	*Harvest and Harvesting* (Cambridge U.P.).
Orwin, C. S.	*A History of English Farming* (Nelson).
Quennell, C. H. B. & M.	*Everyday Life Series* (Batsford).
	A History of Everyday Things Series (Batsford).
Symon, J. A.	*Scottish Farming Past and Present* (Oliver and Boyd).
Trow-Smith, R.	*Life from the Land* (Longmans).
Whitlock, R.	*A Short History of Farming* (Baker).
Wright, P.	*Old Farm Implements* (Black).

Index

Numbers in **bold type** refer to the figure numbers of the illustrations.